THE MAN CAVE

THE MAN CAVE

finding your secret sanctuary
for life development

MICHAEL A PENDER SR.

New York

THE MAN CAVE
finding your secret sanctuary for life development

© 2016 **MICHAEL A PENDER SR..**

Published in New York, New York, by Morgan James Publishing. Morgan James and The Entrepreneurial Publisher are trademarks of Morgan James, LLC.
www.MorganJamesPublishing.com

The Morgan James Speakers Group can bring authors to your live event. For more information or to book an event visit The Morgan James Speakers Group at www.TheMorganJamesSpeakersGroup.com.

A **free** eBook edition is available with the purchase of this print book.

CLEARLY PRINT YOUR NAME ABOVE IN UPPER CASE

Instructions to claim your free eBook edition:
1. Download the BitLit app for Android or iOS
2. Write your name in **UPPER CASE** on the line
3. Use the BitLit app to submit a photo
4. Download your eBook to any device

ISBN 978-1-63047-553-6 paperback
ISBN 978-1-63047-554-3 eBook
ISBN 978-1-63047-555-0 hardcover
Library of Congress Control Number:
2015901709

Cover Design by:
Ryan Rhoades

Interior Design by:
Bonnie Bushman

In an effort to support local communities and raise awareness and funds, Morgan James Publishing donates a percentage of all book sales for the life of each book to Habitat for Humanity Peninsula and Greater Williamsburg

Get involved today, visit
www.MorganJamesBuilds.com

Habitat for Humanity®
Peninsula and
Greater Williamsburg
Building Partner

TABLE OF CONTENTS

FOREWORD

You hold in your hand a book that could well be a key given to you by God to open up the door to the exciting and meaningful future God has planned for your life.

When a young boy named Michael Pender stepped on a green and white bus sent to his doorstep from a local church by a God that loved him and sent His only Son Jesus to set him free from the bondage of sin, he had no idea of the joy and victories that were set before him. God had a plan for Michael like He has a plan for you. Michael immediately realized God had something special He wanted him to do and God is not finished yet with that purpose.

This book you are about to read is an answer to your prayers or the prayers of someone who wants God to use you. God blessed me by allowing me to be Michael's first pastor. But, in addition, He has let me witness up close what God can do with a young boy who forsakes all to follow Christ and submit to the perfect will of his Heavenly Father.

Today is the first day of the rest of your life. This book could well be one of the greatest blessings of your life in helping to conform you into the image of our Lord and Savior Jesus Christ.

—**John D. Morgan**, Senior Pastor
Sagemont Church
Houston, Texas

ACKNOWLEDGEMENT

To Fallbrook's mighty men of valor and the sons I passionately adore, may the words in this book equip, instruct, exhort, correct and empower you for service in God's kingdom.

INTRODUCTION

"So David departed from there and escaped to the cave of Adullam, and when his brothers and all his father's household heard of it, they went down there to him. Everyone who was in distress, and everyone who was in debt, and everyone who was discontented gathered to him; and he became captain over them. Now there were about four hundred men with him."

1 Samuel 22:1-2

Today, a man cave is described as a male sanctuary, a room or other area in a home that is primarily a male sanctuary. It is designed and furnished to accommodate the man's recreational activities, hobbies, etc. This book will introduce you to the original man cave – one that had a total different purpose and perspective for all mankind.

Thousands of years ago, David was in very much need of a "modern day" man cave. As a child, this soon-to-be king was filled with the Holy Spirit after the Prophet Samuel anointed him. David later became a great military commander, but he could not rescue himself from Saul and ultimately was forced into seclusion to save his life.

David's confinement to the cave of Adullam was out of desperation, as he lived in hiding from Saul, who sought to kill him. But this once cold, damp and dark shelter became a place of earnest supplication for David. In the book, take refuge with David to see how he turned his cave of despair and hopelessness into a "Center for Life Development" – a place that God used to change not only his personal life but the lives of thousands who ultimately found themselves retreating there.

ADULLAM'S CAVE

Moonlight splashed counterfeit warmth onto the damp cave walls. The inhabitant of the cave found little comfort in the stoic setting. He rubbed his hands together, resisting the cold night air that rippled through his body. David was unsure whether it was his plight, or his new environment, that shook him with chills. The cave had been occupied before; it stank of dead animal flesh and human filth. David never envisioned his kingship leading him from the wealth of a palace into lonely destitution. Samuel never spoke of this in his prophecy. Saul was a maniac. God appointed him king. He never asked for it, yet he was running for his life from the King of all Israel. He knew better than to question God's will. Men—both modern and historical—desire a sign or sense of being sure about the next step. Wrestling with his situation, he reluctantly dropped his head back against the damp cave wall to seek the face of God. He closed his eyes and prayed, "Not my will God, but your will."

CHAPTER ONE

DAVID'S MAN CAVE

man cave

noun Informal.

a room or other area in a home that is primarily a male sanctuary, designed and furnished to accommodate the man's recreational activities, hobbies, etc.: The basement is my husband's man cave—during football season, you can usually find him down there watching the game with his buddies on the big-screen TV. [1]

A man cave is a place of refuge for men, away from the wife, kids, and family dog. It is a sanctuary of peace and privacy. Its provocative theme is, "What happens in the man cave stays in the man cave." It is a place where a

---

1   http://dictionary.reference.com/browse/man+cave?s=t

man can solve the problems of the world from his couch. Every man can safely be a reclining chair quarterback without injury (and without the millions of dollars). That is a man cave in the hands of the common man. However, if you desire something powerful and uncommon, use the solitude to seek God.

At this time Saul was king—Israel's first. God had ruled over Israel before its inhabitants asked Him for an earthly king. The neighboring nations had kings. The people of Israel were cynical about the Prophet Samuel's sons as leaders. So God granted them their request with the disclaimer that they would suffer taxation and be subject to the control and whims of their king. Let's take a look at what God said about this change in leadership.

> *So Samuel spoke all the words of the LORD to the people who had asked of him a king. He said, "This will be the procedure of the king who will reign over you: he will take your sons and place them for himself in his chariots and among his horsemen and they will run before his chariots. "He will appoint for himself commanders of thousands and of fifties, and some to do his plowing and to reap his harvest and to make his weapons of war and equipment for his chariots. "He will also take your daughters for perfumers and cooks and bakers. "He will take the best of your fields and your vineyards and your olive groves and give them to his servants. "He will take a tenth of your seed and of your vineyards and give to his officers and to his servants. "He will also take your male servants and your*

*female servants and your best young men and your donkeys
and use them for his work. "He will take a tenth of your
flocks, and you yourselves will become his servants." Then
you will cry out in that day because of your king whom you
have chosen for yourselves, but the LORD will not answer
you in that day."*

1st Samuel 8:10 - 18 NASB

So the hardening of the people's heart toward Saul's regime
was inevitable. God had warned His children that having a
human king could not replace having Him as their leader. Saul's
human capacity to sin made him a prime candidate for his fall
from grace.

King David, Saul's replacement, spent a huge portion of
his leadership training in dismal caves. Damp caves offered
darkness and shelter to cover him from enemies and weather,
but little comfort. Saul, the first King of Israel, was in hot
pursuit of David because God handed over the crown to him.
Saul's heart raged with jealousy and a blinding vendetta which
resulted in his madness. Thirty years of his reign were spent
seeking to destroy his perceived enemy, searching relentlessly in
the hills and failing to capture David.

David fled when he was convinced that his life was in
danger. First, he went to Nob to Ahimelech the priest. Then, he
fled to Gath, to the house of King Achish where his life was also
in danger. David faked craziness in order to escape King Achish.
Then, he sought refuge in the cave of Adullam. Here's where we
will start our journey:

> *So David departed from there and escaped to the cave*
> *of Adullam; and when his brothers and all his father's*
> *household heard of it, they went down there to him.*
> *Everyone who was in distress, and everyone who was in*
> *debt, and everyone who was discontented gathered to him;*
> *and he became captain over them. Now there were about*
> *four hundred men with him.*

(1 Samuel 22:1-2 NASB)

I want to begin this section with questions. What led David into his man cave at Adullam? What were the circumstances surrounding his hasty departure from Gibeah? David was a fugitive running for his life from Saul's violent pursuit. Later in that same chapter, Saul murdered all of the priests of Nob. Saul's servant was there in Nob while David was with the priests. The servant acted as an informant about David's visit. All of the priests, men, women, and children in the city were executed. David had every reason to flee for his life. Saul had previously tried to kill David six times.

While running away, David decided he needed a better plan. He said, "Well let me go to the city of Gath," which was the hometown of Goliath. David killed Goliath, which infuriated the Philistines. It may sound strange that David would seek refuge in a city of the enemy. He may have thought that Saul would no longer pursue him because he was residing in the city of his enemies, the Philistines. So David fled to Gath but he miscalculated the level of hatred the Philistines had toward him. When the situation got out of control, he pretended to be a maniac. The Bible says that he allowed foam to come out of his mouth, to seem like he was insane. This allowed David the opportunity to escape from the city. After he had left Gath, David found himself alone in his man cave in Adullam.

David experienced a major adjustment in his efforts to preserve his life. He left everything that he knew in the palace of Saul. He ended up in the dark recesses of a cave that lacked all the comforts of home, including his wife Michal. God used this place to build up David from a military commander to a king. David's man cave was a center for life development, which is a contrast to a university setting or biblical training center. David's man cave was not a seminary; it was not a place where holy scriptures were studied. It was a center for Godly life development where his family and four hundred distressed, discontented, and deeply in debt men assembled because they believed in his kingship. The Bible describes why his family came to the cave. His family needed to come because Saul was paranoid and killing anything close to David. If Saul found David was in a certain area, Saul would murder innocent people in the city that hosted his archenemy. David's family joined him in the cave for their own safety and to lend support.

The men who came to the man cave were the outcasts of Israel, but they boldly became castaways in a foreign land because of their disillusionment with Israel's first king. They were the citizens who feared Saul's police state leadership style. When he lost his anointing because of his disobedience, God rejected him. He became violently psychotic and a very harsh ruler. These four hundred men came from under that form of leadership.

They were tired of it, they were in debt, discontented and distressed. Here is a closer look at the state of mind that these men were in:

- *Debt*: During this time in the world, being in debt could ruin a man and cost him his life. He could lose his property, be sold into slavery, or lose his family to slavery as a result.
- *Discontented:* Men often lose heart and hope in the midst of unjust leadership. They were broken because their dreams had been demolished and success had escaped them under the current regime.
- *Distress:* Some of these men had somehow gotten on the wrong side of Saul and were persecuted and oppressed. Perhaps they would not conform, or they spoke openly about their distress under his leadership.

These men left Israel behind and went to where David was because they were seeking Godly leadership. Now when these men came to David's man cave, he focused on God-centered life development to transform these outcasts into mighty men of God.

I believe that this is one of the areas where we sometimes fail as the Church. We fall short in providing people with opportunity. We could provide better Godly life development to support victorious, Christ-centered lives. It is imperative that the church equips the body to live life after they are exposed to the word of God. The question every man should ask himself is, "How do I apply this to make my life better for the Lord?" When they look at the church, they should find a living testimony that confirms the word of God. David modeled Godly leadership in the man cave, and his men chose to follow his example.

life development center
noun
a place where men go to be turned into kings of their cave (home), calling, community, and country.

David's man cave was very successful in turning Israel's castaways into skilled and disciplined soldiers, committed to fighting against their country's enemies. His training methods were different. It was rather peculiar how David's four hundred men assembled and developed their mission. Since they were disenfranchised from Israel, one might think that they decided to rise against Israel. However, the Bible reveals otherwise. In this chapter of 1 Samuel and the following, they are not fighting against Israel, but assembling to fight against Israel's enemies. They were like the black soldiers during the darker time of American history.

History records that they were not respected in this country, though they were fighting and dying like the soldiers who were being honored. I consider that rather peculiar. Can you think of another people group that would sacrifice their lives for a country that did not honor the sacrifice? For example, during the American Revolution, the first person to die on the battlefield was Crispus Attucks, a black man who was fighting for America's liberty. He was willing to fight and die for this country even though afterwards, win or lose, he was going back into slavery. Many black men came after him in the Civil War, World War I and II, and the Vietnam War. They laid down their lives for a country that did not love them. So don't count it strange that this happened in David's time. Even exiled men can have a sense of duty and honor to their country.

There were David's men: ostracized from their country and still fighting for their nation. No matter what you feel about our country, it is never okay to engage in home-grown terrorism. It is never okay to plot destruction against your country. We have to realize that as Americans, God has placed us here and blessed us. We should be willing to fight and try to make this country a better place. So here we have David and his four hundred castaways. The man of God develops a training program based on the experience he acquired as a military leader prior to being exiled.

The church must commit to being a Davidic man cave where the distressed, discontented, and deeply indebted people assemble to be transformed into mighty people of God. For example, as patriarchs in the local church, we should advocate creating a place where our young girls can come when some of them get pregnant and have nowhere to go. Societal statistics and mores indicate that some of our young girls are going to get pregnant. The bottom line is that we cannot walk around merely saying, "Well that's a shame they're getting pregnant." Yes, it is a shame they are getting pregnant. However, we have a responsibility to create Godly environments in which we can support them in becoming mighty women of God. We must also train up that girl in the way she should go, according to the Word of God. David wasn't interested in throwing away the castaways. He was trying to use the castaways for the Glory of God. Do you know we have to do the same thing? We've got to begin to use those that society wants to reject.

Remember David's man cave was not a seminary. Nor was he hosting a regular Bible study that you would often experience at a church. He was not the high priest. David was a military officer at this point working for Saul. He was not a spiritual leader of Israel. He was a skilled warrior, a man of battle filled with courage and leadership. The cave was not a place for expanding Bible knowledge. It was a safe place for the outcasts—for those who were rejected and unhappy. He took responsibility and initiative to gather and build up people with imperfect lives. The army that God had provided to battle alongside David was basically a hand full of vagabonds. But they had some other qualities that we will be discovering in upcoming chapters.

400 MEN AND COUNTING

The sun was peeking over the new day's horizon as David rises from his prostate position of prayer. He grabs his musty cloak from the damp cold floor of the cave, reluctantly. Oh how he wished he could stay in the presence of the Lord a little longer. The men just kept coming, from all over Israel, he had counted over 400 last night and the cave was almost at its capacity. What was it that God expected of him? These men were novices in the art of war at best. He let out a sigh of resignation. But they loved God and they trusted him. Whatever it was that God was doing in him, he would teach it to his men, they were in need of instruction so he would turn this cave into a place of life development. His heart agreed with this mission and he set out that very day to accomplish it.

CHAPTER TWO

THE LIFE DEVELOPMENT CENTER

ere we will peer into the Cave of Adullam to observe the inner operations of David's *Center for Spiritual Life Development.* To review, we will look at 1 Samuel 22:1 – 2.

So David departed from there and escaped to the cave of Adullam; and when his brothers and all his father's household heard of it, they went down there to him. Everyone who was in distress, and everyone who was in debt, and everyone who was discontented gathered to him; and he became captain over them. Now there were about four hundred men with him.

David was on the run from Saul and he found himself at the cave of Adullam. It takes a true man of God to turn a dark and forbidding situation into something that brings glory to God. David was the man of the hour and God had anointed him to be king, regardless of his residence. Through David's time in harsh places like the cave of Adullam, the Lord shaped and refined him in the natural sense. The cave of Adullam was also used by God as a Center of Spiritual Life Development for David to grow stronger spiritually, as well. In Psalm 57 and 142, we get a firsthand account of his experience there. Let's take a closer look at Psalm 57 because it accurately reveals the spiritual impact David's cave days had on his life. In this psalm we see how God used the cave of Adullam to stimulate in David, prayer to God, faith in God, and praise for God.

> *Be gracious to me, O God, be gracious to me, For my soul takes refuge in You; And in the shadow of Your wings I will take refuge Until destruction passes by. I will cry to God Most High.*

Psalm 57: 1 - 2a

Early on in the psalm, it is evident that the Lord used David's difficult experience in the cave of Adullam as a teaching experience to establish open communication. The cave removed David from his most loyal friend Jonathan. So while he was away, David learned to share his most difficult days with the Lord. Prayer was much more to David than just asking God for things, it was a place where he shared his life with God. Like David, our prayers must be bigger than asking, they must be rooted in sharing our entire lives with God. Ask yourself, who are you sharing your life with? Your spouse, your friends, and your children? If so, you have a good start. How much of your life are you sharing with God, though? David's communication with God strengthened and equipped him for the challenges he faced. Could you use that kind of help in your life?

The Lord also used David's experience in the cave of Adullam to stimulate his faith. He removed David from all of his earthly supports and comforts, which caused David to rely on God alone.

To God who accomplishes all things for me. He will send from heaven and save me;

He reproaches him who tramples upon me. Selah. God will send forth His lovingkindness and His truth.

Psalm 57: 2b – 3

Psalm 57: 1-3 reveals that David's faith at the cave became greater than his troubles. We need to start rolling like David – where our faith during hard times is greater than our troubles. Our troubles don't have to conquer us; we are more than conquerors.

The Lord also used David's experience in the cave of Adullam to stimulate his praise. Psalm 57: 7-10 reveals his yearning to praise God in the midst of it all.

My heart is steadfast, O God, my heart is steadfast; I will sing, yes, I will sing praises! Awake, my glory! Awake, harp and lyre! I will awaken the dawn. I will give thanks to You, O Lord, among

*the peoples; I will sing praises to You among the nations. For Your
lovingkindness is great to the heavens And Your truth to the clouds.
Be exalted above the heavens, O God; Let Your glory be above all
the earth.*

Let's take a detailed look at verses 7 through 11 to glean
from the Great Music Director of Praise.

- Verse 7 – 8 declares that David is spiritually and
  physically prepared for praise. Are you prepared to
  praise God regardless of the situation?
- Verse 9 reveals his praise will include going public for
  the world to see (not just in your private prayer closet
  or in church services).
- Verse 10 reveals "why" he praised God. What is your
  "why" for praising God?
- Verse 11 reveals where he wanted God to be in his life
  (Lord or Underling). Where do you want God to be
  in your life?

In sports, one of the hardest things, both mentally and
physically, is changing direction. Spiritually, one of the hardest
things is changing your thought direction from problems to
praises. David avoided tunnel vision by concentrating on God
more than his problems. He simply changed his focus.

Imagine yourself in David's shoes—in a very uncomfortable
place. David kept a posture of surrender to God's will, even
in this place of discontent, so that he could train and equip
the outcasts of his nation. His training began in the sheep
pasture. He was ruler over the minor things before he became

ruler over many. Evidence of his relationship development with God is established when he fights Goliath and kills the giant that had all Israel's mighty military commanders shaking in their boots. So David was no stranger to the battlefield or leadership. The cave of Adullam was the training ground for his crown.

In this cave, David shared what he had learned on the battlefield of life with those whom society considered derelicts and malcontents. They were not from the Who's Who List of the Israeli society register. David's cave code was consistent with God's selection process. He does not call someone into service based on their being great and powerful. He looks at the heart of a man and checks to see if it beats for Him. David's training for his men was God-centered, based on spiritual lessons he learned from the Holy Spirit. His men were diamonds in the rough. To the common man with natural vision they were worthless and could easily be overlooked by the untrained eye. Like diamonds in their natural state, David's men were uncut and unpolished so their exceptional characteristics were hidden. David's spiritually charged sight saw extraordinary diamonds that needed the Master's touch to make them stand out in the crowd.

I love to be the underdog for a couple of reasons. There isn't a whole lot of pressure to perform because nobody thinks you can do anything. They might think you are dumb. What they fail to understand is that God's assessment of us is far more important than other people's opinions. Based on my casual appearance most of the time, you wouldn't think I was a pastor. At the end of the day, what difference does it make if you walk around town and everybody knows you? Your reputation precedes you and you are honored in your community. But what if you go somewhere where you are virtually unknown and people refuse to make eye contact with you and validate your presence with a "hello"? Does that change God's potential in you or his purpose for your life? The answer is undeniably no.

> *For consider your calling, brethren, that there were not many wise according to the flesh, not many mighty, not many noble; but God has chosen the foolish things of the world to shame the wise, and God has chosen the weak things of the world to shame the things which are strong, and the base things of the world and the despised God has chosen, the things that are not, so that He may nullify the things that are, so that no man may boast before God.*
>
> 1 Corinthians 1: 26 -29

We don't ever want to get it twisted because often we want to look for those that look and dress the part. They only look like they "got it going on." I learned a long time ago that some people who are dressing like they are rich, driving like they are rich, and living like they are rich, don't have a dime to their name. They are living paycheck to paycheck, stressed out behind closed doors. They are going crazy because they don't know how they will pay for that fancy car. Don't be fooled by appearances.

There is a place for everyone in the kingdom. For those who worked hard all their life and have accumulated a lot of things, there's a place for you. You've been disciplined since you were in high school. You ordered your life. You did your homework and you were on point and God blessed you. I'm proud of you and glad for your success, there's a place for you in the kingdom of God. Society knows that is true but God says that He also has a place for the people who are considered the misfits of the world. There's a place for the person who didn't do any homework. You were in school and you were partying, acting crazy and you were doing your thing. As a result, you don't have a diploma now and you may have served some time in jail. Your life is all kind of messed up because of those poor choices that you made. You don't think there's a place for you in society. Sometimes we think that the only people in this world who belong are those that have it all together. I'm not knocking them— praise God they got it right earlier. I pray that all young people will realize that if you get it earlier you can enjoy life longer.

If you didn't get it early, be encouraged because God wants to use you too. God has big plans for you, as well. David's cave was open for the rejects. Prior to his cave experience, David was rejected by his family. When God told Samuel to go to Jesse's house to anoint the next king of Israel, he paraded all of his sons before the prophet except one: David. At the time, David was out tending sheep. Can you imagine the surprise of Jesse's household when Samuel poured anointing oil on David's head? He was the chosen one, but to the natural eye he was just a sheep herder. It took God's commission ceremony for the world to see David's potential.

David and his men were diamonds in the rough. What is a diamond in the rough?

diamond in the rough
phrase of <u>diamond</u>
1. North American
a person who is generally of good character but lacks manners, education, or style.[2]

A naturally occurring diamond starts out like a lump of coal. After exposure to extreme pressure and high temperatures, the lump becomes something special. Then it is mined, polished, and precision-cut before eventually being placed in a jewelry store. They can be overlooked and considered worthless to an untrained person. Those of you who are untrained in what natural diamonds look like—imagine that I'd put you in a cave somewhere. You might see some small stones without ever realizing they were real diamonds. Our perception of a diamond is what some of you have on your finger. You may think that diamonds "sparkle" beautifully in their naturally occurring state. But the diamond on your finger has been cut and polished.

There are some people in this world who are not, as of yet, cut or polished. Some people get it early—they were cut and polished at a young age. I praise God for those 15- and 16-year-olds who get it early and stay disciplined because they got cut and polished at an early age. Then some of you are 45 years old and still in a rough state. You're just as raw as the

---

2   http://www.oxforddictionaries.com/definition/english/rough-diamond

day you showed up at the cave. You've been in church all your life, uncut and unpolished, but in God's eyes you still have diamond potential.

You're just as much a diamond as the ones who are cut and polished. There is nothing less authentic about you. The only difference is that they were cut and polished. So you know what God is waiting to do with some of you today? He's simply waiting to start the refining process in your life!

You may be saying to God, "You don't know how many babies I've had! You don't know how many women or men I've been with! You don't know why my finances are this way!" It doesn't matter, because God just wants to cut and polish you through a series of changes. God can cut and polish you to where nobody recognizes the old you. Don't let anyone tell you that it's not possible. If you are a believer, don't let anyone convince you that you are less than a diamond. Even in your naturally occurring state, you can say "I'm a diamond, I just waited a little bit longer to get cut and polished." Realize that all you have to do is come to God and say, "Lord, start cutting on me, start polishing me."

Start cutting on me so I can be a better husband. Start polishing me so I can be a better wife. Start cutting on me so I can be a better student. If we would only come to God, fall on our face before Him and say, "Oh Lord, cut me, polish me! Get me ready!" He would do it!

David's men were diamonds in the rough and David said, "Come on in." The rest of the world was looking over them because their eyes were untrained to recognize God-given potential. David had supernatural vision because God had anointed and empowered him to see what the common man could not see. Those four hundred unwanted dudes joined David at the cave of Adullam. He began to cut and polish them for kingdom work. Do you know what they did? They protected the hills of Judah. Saul did not protect his own kingdom. He wouldn't protect all of it. The unprotected areas in the hills were the parts nobody wanted to protect. David's mighty men saw the necessity to lend a helping hand around the communities everyone gave up on. They said to the Philistines, "You can't have this area! It belongs to Israel and we're going to defend it." Four hundred men who were cut and polished became soldiers. Nobody recognized them, but after they were trained for God, they shined bright like the diamonds He intended them to be. I don't care where you are today. It doesn't matter to God. Just let him start cutting on you and polishing you. You will be capable of amazing things for His glory.

PSALM 91

As David contemplated the danger and all that he had been given charge over, a song of safety inspired by God, came to his mind. He hastily grabbed something to record this declaration of faith …

He that dwelleth in the secret place of the Most High Shall abide under the shadow of the Almighty.

I will say of Jehovah, He is my refuge and my fortress; My God, in whom I trust.

For he will deliver thee from the snare of the fowler, And from the deadly pestilence.

He will cover thee with his pinions, And under his wings shalt thou take refuge: His truth is a shield and a buckler.

Thou shalt not be afraid for the terror by night, Nor for the arrow that flieth by day;

For the pestilence that walketh in darkness, Nor for the destruction that wasteth at noonday.

A thousand shall fall at thy side, And ten thousand at thy right hand; But it shall not come nigh thee.

Only with thine eyes shalt thou behold, And see the reward of the wicked.

For thou, O Jehovah, art my refuge! Thou hast made the Most High thy habitation;

There shall no evil befall thee, Neither shall any plague come nigh thy tent.

For he will give his angels charge over thee, To keep thee in all thy ways.

They shall bear thee up in their hands, Lest thou dash thy foot against a stone.

Thou shalt tread upon the lion and adder: The young lion and the serpent shalt thou trample under foot.

Because he hath set his love upon me, therefore will I deliver him: I will set him on high, because he hath known my name.

He shall call upon me, and I will answer him; I will be with him in trouble: I will deliver him, and honor him.

With long life will I satisfy him, And show him my salvation.

CHAPTER THREE

THE MAN CAVE POSTURE OF SAFETY

safety

noun

1. the state of being safe; freedom from the occurrence or risk of injury, danger, or loss.
2. the quality of averting or not causing injury, danger, or loss.
3. a contrivance or device to prevent injury or avert danger.
4. Also called lock, safety catch, safety lock. a locking or cutoff device that prevents a gun from being fired accidentally.
5. the action of keeping safe.[3]

---

3   http://dictionary.reference.com/browse/safety?s=t

David's man cave was a center for life development where he took over 400 vagabonds and turned the world as they knew it upside down. I want to lay out a couple of things about this center for life development. One, David's man cave, the campus for this center for life development, provided safety. If we're going to use man caves as centers for life development, we need to have some rules. Safety was a priority in David's man cave because it needed to be safe from Saul. If given a chance, Saul would've killed David, his family, and the 400 castaways.

David's experience with Saul taught him to be proactive, not merely reactionary, regarding safety. People often wait until something bad happens before they start to implement safety measures that will protect them. The church must be proactive when it comes to safety. It ought to be a safe haven. We shouldn't be scared or worried when we come to a place of worship. Let me share with you a powerful scripture. Let's look at verses 21-23 in that same chapter:

> *He told David that Saul had killed the priests of the LORD. Then David said to Abiathar, "That day, when Doeg the Edomite was there, I knew he would be sure to tell Saul. I am responsible for the death of your whole family. Stay with me; don't be afraid. The man who wants to kill you is trying to kill me too. You will be safe with me."*

I like what David said. And what David said is what I believe every single leader in the church ought to be able to say. Let's look at verse 21. Abiathar told David that Saul had killed the priest of the Lord. Abiathar just lost his father and every other priest that he knew because Saul murdered all of them. He sent Doeg the Edomite to kill them, so he lost everybody. He lost his whole community—every man, woman and child. He was the lone survivor. Then David said to Abiathar, "I knew on that day when Doeg the Edomite was there that he would surely report my whereabouts to Saul." He felt that he'd brought about the death of every person in Nob. David felt bad about going to Nob and getting assistance because Saul misinterpreted the role that the priests played in his escape.

Verse 23 is a very important verse when determining if a person in leadership has the heart of God in regards to His people. If anyone in leadership can't say this and mean it in their heart, they need to resign. David said "stay with me." "Do not be afraid for he who seeks my life seeks your life," and these last six words are so important, "for you are safe with me." David was committed to making sure he was providing safety spiritually, physically, mentally, financially, and morally.

Abiathar didn't have to worry about his food, clothing or shelter. He didn't have to worry about being violated in any way while in David's care. Don't build a Sunday school class if the group can't be safe with you. Don't say you want to teach in the singles ministry if folk can't be safe with you. Don't say you want to preach if the folk can't be safe with you. If the members can't be safe with you, you ought not to be a leader in anybody's church.

People have to see the church as a safe haven and a safety net. As a pastor of a church, shouldn't you be safe with me? Shouldn't you be able to come to my office without me making a pass at you? For that matter, shouldn't you be able to go into any pastors' office and not be afraid that you will be compromised in any way? Think about it. Shouldn't your money be safe in your local church and you have no fear that the pastor is stealing your money? Shouldn't your children be safe in this atmosphere from predators? David was saying, "You're safe with me, safe on every front." Any church that seeks to become a Life Development Center and open a Davidic man cave has to make safety a priority. You may ask the question, "why?" Sometimes the church has been one of the greatest places to manipulate and take advantage of people.

You know why? Folk come here all the time distressed, in debt and discontented. It's a prime opportunity for those that don't want to do right to manipulate others. God has created the church as a spiritual hospital, to be able to minister to those who are hurting. Some take advantage of the people in the church who are weak, worried, and wanting help by prostituting their temporary status in life for personal gain. It's a great place to do that. Some people that come to church on a regular basis do not have a Godly agenda. They're on the prowl looking for somebody that they can get.

For example: A lady is having a hard time and she's feeling lonely. There will always be somebody in the building just waiting for her to cry on his shoulder. I share this story about my son, just to show you what goes on in the world. I was somewhere with my son, that is commonly frequented by people who have the world's view on life. A young lady who was engaged said hello to everybody. I was introduced as my son's father, not just his friend but his father. She went over to him and looked at his face and asked, "How old are you?" He said, "I'm 18." She proceeded to say after peering at him for a short time, "You are delicious!" It scared me because that's my son. I didn't know he was delicious.

What I want you to know is this, there are people that come to church, just waiting for an opportunity to look at you and say you're delicious. If somebody's bold enough to say that in front of a young man's father, they are bold enough to come to church looking for delicious prospects. We live in a different world and the church has to be committed to being safe from the Saul's of this world. We are responsible for providing spiritual, physical, mental, financial and moral safety for the men, women, and children, God commends into our care.

Now let's take a closer look at David's strategy for protecting those who were entrusted to Him by God. According to the scriptures David intimately knew the source of his safety. In Psalm 4:8 David tells God that "In peace I will both lie down and sleep, For You alone, O LORD, make me to dwell in safety." Another example is seen in Psalm 27:5, "For in the day of trouble He will conceal me in His tabernacle; In the secret place of His tent He will hide me; He will lift me up on a rock."

David also made sure that his family was safe. When David was worried about the safety of his parents, he went to Mizpah in Moab. David asked permission from the king to allow his father and mother to stay under royal protection until he came into his own kingdom.

He cared for the safety of his men as evidenced in his conversation with Abiathar. He also cared about their families. Once while away in battle, David's camp was raided by the

Amalekites who burned it to the ground and took the women and children. David's men were so distraught that he thought they would stone him, but God strengthened him and they went to the enemy's camp and recovered all.

David also had a compassionate heart for his constituents. He was concerned for their safety. He established a reputation as an excellent warrior throughout all the land, and those who fought with him were also skilled warriors. With a reputation of this sort, enemies think twice about trying to take possession of your kingdom. Once his kingdom was safely established in Israel, David sent for the Ark of the Covenant. It was placed at the home of Obededom. His original plan to move the Ark resulted in the death of Uzzah, because he did not follow God's protocol. He did not move it again until he was assured that he could do it without harming his people.

Just as it was important during David's reign, it is equally important now for the church to be a safe place. Church leadership should place the safety of their flock as a high priority when running a spiritual life development center. With everything that is happening in the world today, people who are distressed, in debt, and discontented need a place of refuge. The church should be that place.

DISCIPLINE BASED INSTRUCTION

Some of the men considered him to be a harsh taskmaster, but if they were going to fight for God, they needed discipline. It was a great refining tool, especially for men who had nowhere else to go. He'd watched the others chastise the men who were reluctant to follow orders. When he'd served as Commander and Chief of Saul's army that was not the case. Those men were more competitive in nature, but these men just wanted to please him and please their God. What a gift!

"David went to Nob, to Ahimelek the priest. Ahimelek trembled when he met him, and asked, "Why are you alone? Why is no one with you?"

David answered Ahimelek the priest, "The king sent me on a mission and said to me, 'No one is to know anything about the mission I am sending you on.' As for my men, I have told them to meet me at a certain place. Now then,

what do you have on hand? Give me five loaves of bread, or whatever you can find."

But the priest answered David, "I don't have any ordinary bread on hand; however, there is some consecrated bread here—provided the men have kept themselves from women."

David replied, "Indeed women have been kept from us, as usual whenever I set out. The men's bodies are holy even on missions that are not holy. How much more so today!" So the priest gave him the consecrated bread, since there was no bread there except the bread of the Presence that had been removed from before the Lord and replaced by hot bread on the day it was taken away."(NIV)

CHAPTER FOUR

THE MAN CAVE POSTURE OF DISCIPLINE

pleasure based

noun

a disproportionate emphasis on pleasure and leisure opposed to hard work and self-denial.

David's man cave wasn't pleasure based. There's a disproportionate emphasis placed on pleasure and leisure opposed to hard work and self-denial in our current society. We are a pleasure and leisure based civilization. As a consumer driven society, we focus on buying products and things that go faster and make us feel better. We tend to not care much about hard work and self-denial. Individuals run from jobs where they've got to work hard, trying to find one where they don't have to be as industrious.

If you had a choice between a job where you worked hard and one that you aren't required to exert as much effort, most people would want to find a job where they have to do literally next to nothing. They often miss out on the rewarding experience of working hard and seeing the fruit of their diligence. Hard work also allows you the privilege of expanding and growing your skill set to mastery of a task. So when we choose the easy way out, we often get short term results and a limited reward.

In light of the condition of his men when they arrived and made David their captain, it's not surprising that his man cave wasn't pleasure based. They weren't sitting around playing dominos all day. If those 400 men came and they had all their dominos, their cars, their basketballs, their golf bags and their footballs, it wouldn't have been room in the cave for them. If they brought all their stuff with them, David would have to command them to leave all of that stuff outside the cave. It was not time to play, but to get ready for battle.

You know what I've realized? In order to combat this complacency in our neighborhoods, we've got to get these dudes that are sitting around playing dominos all day long somewhere to get some training. We've got to develop them to become mighty men of God. I noticed that there is a distinct difference between men and women. A woman will sit around her friends and they'll talk about the deeper things in life. Men will avoid deep reflective conversations. I'm guilty of this and many of you are also. Women will sit down and talk about intimate feminine stuff without caution. I'm not trying to make light of this because they are just communicating in a way that best fits the way they are wired. It doesn't mean anything to them but if we happen to be close enough to overhear their conversation, we'll be like, "What did you just say?"

Men, what we do is we often spend a lot of time on just meaningless stuff. You let me play basketball and have a good day and hit 25 or 30 points. I'm going to talk about that probably for the next four years. Every chance I get to see another dude I'm going to tell him about it. I'm going to talk about that until Jesus gets back. Ladies are different. They sit down to talk and get around to all kinds of important stuff. Men, we've got to get beyond the trivial, the meaningless chatter and do like David did and get down to the "nitty gritty" on what's going to help us get better in this life we are living for the Lord.

Our conversations have to change. They must get deeper. We need to be on the phone discussing deeper stuff. Why? That's how we're going to grow and get better in the things of God. You see David wasn't interested in a pleasure based system, but he was interested in a disciplined based system. David was a great leader who understood the importance of discipline and transforming castaways. Check this out. I want to share with you just a few more scriptures.

This is another powerful revelation just to show you how David was committed to discipline. These dudes were disciplined. They weren't out of order. They weren't walking and playing around all day. They were disciplined soldiers, who worked on their craft on and off the field of battle.

In 1 Samuel 24, we see a different side of Saul. It's a little bit funny so I'll try to show you some of the humorous side of this passage. It says *"when Saul returned from pursuing the Philistines he was told – said behold, David is in the wilderness of En Gedi.*

Then Saul took 3000 chosen men from all of Israel and went to seek David and his men and the front of the rocks of the wild goats. He came to the sheep fold on the way where there was a cave."

Remember David and his crew were used to hanging out in a cave. They knew every nuance about cave dwelling. So they were there in the cave when Saul went inside to relieve himself, no not a number one but a number two. It's in the text, I'm not making this up. Now David and his men were already sitting in the inner recesses of the cave. Now remember, these were the same dudes that hated Saul. They were ready to throw down. They just didn't like Saul.

Remember what the Bible said, they were distressed, indebted, and discontented. They didn't like his administration and now they're thinking, it's finally time for us to get revenge. In verse 4, David's men said, *"Behold this is the day in which the Lord sends to you, 'Behold; I'm about to give your enemy into your hand and you shall do to him as it seems good to you. Then David arose, cut off the edge of Saul's robe secretly. It came about afterwards that David's conscience bothered him because he had cut off the edge of Saul's robe."*

In verses 6 and 7, we see where his leadership stood out, so David said, *"Far be it from me because the Lord that I shall do this thing to my lord."* Why? Saul was David's lord. Lower case L, because he was not his God, but he was his leader. He was his king, and in David's words "the Lord's anointed." He refused, *"to stretch out my hand against him, since he is the Lord's anointed. David persuaded his men with these words and did not allow them to rise up against Saul. And Saul arose, left the cave, and went on his way."*

Have you ever seen a mob before? David had these dudes so disciplined that if this had occurred prior to their training program in the life development center Saul would have been dead. But because of their commander-in-chief, when Saul was in the cave with them, David was able to keep them quiet and orderly.

discipline

noun

noun: discipline

1. the practice of training people to obey rules or a code of behavior, using punishment to correct disobedience.[4]

David was a man of great discipline. His soldiers were disciplined. We are naturally bent towards doing things that bring us pleasure. But the fruit of a pursuit of those kind of things is often meaningless and they don't allow growth in our lives. And what we have to do is be committed to discipline and order. Our church is not the church for everyone, some people don't like order and we are careful to do things with a line upon line, precept upon precept mentality. The world we live in is structured. Its creator is a God of structure and order and there ought to be structure and order in the church. Some people have good jobs and because they want to keep those jobs they develop self-control and become proficient in their work assignment so that they can enjoy the benefits of it. Getting a paycheck every week is a huge incentive. Yet, they want to come

---

4   http://www.oxforddictionaries.com/us/definition/american_english/
     discipline

to a church with no order and get to do whatever it is that they want to do. But that's not the will of God. Structure, order and discipline are necessary to live the life God has ordained us to live. The main reason we're losing so many of our kids is because there is no structure, order, and control. We need structure, order and discipline in our lives.

David's man cave wasn't pleasure based. It was discipline based. He had to turn these guys into mighty men of God. And to all the brothers who are reading this book today, please hear me when you begin to help other men that are struggling, they need discipline. These young dudes that are going crazy, they need structure, order and discipline. Don't let them come in your class and hijack your classroom. I'm not going to get mad at you if you're tussling and turning tables over when some dude is trying to take your class and you just only wanted to get it back.

I'm not telling you to go out there and be a bully, but I am telling you we've got to do what we've got to do in order to turn an chaotic environment into an organized safe one. We can't have people just come in and hijack the church. Everyone should be welcomed in God's church. You can come in crazy, but know that you won't leave crazy. It's important that we create an environment that the Holy Spirit has liberty to do what he is assigned to do in the body of Christ. The church is God's hospital for those who have infirmities: spiritually, mentally, and physically. That's why structure, order and discipline are important. We're not playing in God's house. That's what David had and that's how he was able to turn their lives around. Churches have to be the same way, and we've got to implement this life development strategy in the pre-school ministry, the children's ministry, the youth ministry, the men's ministry, the women's ministry, etc.

We live in a world where people really don't want that. They want to do whatever they want to do. If you want to grow and be all that God desires for you to be, the best place for you to be is in a structured, orderly and disciplined environment. I know quite a few young men who listened to a small piece of advice that I gave them and now they have totally different lives. Some would have been knee deep in poverty, in prison, or dead. I saw that they were struggling. They were "off as two left shoes." They weren't mastering life at the time but after our discussion they were able to graduate. I told them, "All you want to do is play too much. You need to take yourself to Uncle Sam's Army, Air Force, Navy or Coast Guard. You need to take yourself somewhere like that." Why? I didn't think they would survive in the real world without the discipline that joining the military affords each new recruit.

For all the parents who are saying "That's my baby. I don't want him to fight in any wars. What if he dies?" We've got more young men dying here than we've got dying over there. Many of them have made some of the biggest mistakes of their lives right in their own neighborhoods. Some of our kids who don't want to do right or act right, need to be escorted down to the recruiter's office and be put under the structure, order and discipline of the armed services. Give them four years to make up their mind and maybe get the player out of their systems. The military will tell them when to wake up, especially since you can't get them up. They sleep until

11:00 am in your house. Anytime you've got a kid at your house sleeping until noon, who doesn't have a job, and you're not trying to get them in Uncle Sam's Army, Navy, Air Force or Marines, you need to drive him down to the recruiter yourself. If you're not you'll be spending your time driving yourself up to the state prison, crying all day long. Why? Our kids need structure, order and discipline.

You might say, "Well you wouldn't do that to your kids." Let me explain something to you. If my son at this very instant, started bugging, tripping and thinking he's delicious and didn't want to go to trade school after high school or go to college or something like that, I would drive him to the recruiter myself. Proverbs 22:15 says, *"Foolishness is bound in the heart of a child; but the rod of correction shall drive it far from him."* The military alternative is the more compassionate "rod of correction," if the other choices are imminent death, a lifetime prison sentence, or perpetual homelessness. None of the others come with a paycheck, food, clothing, or shelter.

I would tell my son, "You better sign that paper and get up out of here." Why? Because I know, his very life depended on him becoming proficient at discipline. David's man cave wasn't pleasure based, but discipline based. We've got to have discipline in our lives as well in order to graduate from the school of life development.

YOU BETTER RECOGNIZE!

Slumped over a dying fire, David is enraged. His men just got back from Nabal's with a report that boils his blood. He refused to offer recompense for their services. "Well, I'll show him, who's the commander and chief of this army of men. We may be outcasts, but you should show some respect for me and my men for protecting your shepherds."

"Now there was a man in Maon whose business was in Carmel; and the man was very rich, and he had three thousand sheep and a thousand goats. And it came about while he was shearing his sheep in Carmel (now the man's name was Nabal, and his wife's name was Abigail. And the woman was intelligent and beautiful in appearance, but the man was harsh and evil in his dealings, and he was a Calebite), that David heard in the wilderness that Nabal was shearing his sheep. So David sent ten young men; and

David said to the young men, "Go up to Carmel, visit Nabal and greet him in my name; and thus you shall say, 'Have a long life, peace be to you, and peace be to your house, and peace be to all that you have. Now I have heard that you have shearers; now your shepherds have been with us and we have not insulted them, nor have they missed anything all the days they were in Carmel. Ask your young men and they will tell you. Therefore let my young men find favor in your eyes, for we have come on a festive day. Please give whatever you find at hand to your servants and to your son David.'

When David's young men came, they spoke to Nabal according to all these words in David's name; then they waited. But Nabal answered David's servants and said, 'Who is David? And who is the son of Jesse? There are many servants today who are each breaking away from his master. Shall I then take my bread and my water and my meat that I have slaughtered for my shearers, and give it to men whose origin I do not know?' So David's young men retraced their way and went back; and they came and told him according to all these words. David said to his men, 'Each of you gird on his sword.' So each man girded on his sword. And David also girded on his sword, and about four hundred men went up behind David while two hundred stayed with the baggage."
(1 Samuel 14:2 – 17)

CHAPTER FIVE

THE MAN CAVE POSTURE OF WALKING IN YOUR ANOINTING

David's man cave was a destitute location where no one would have imagined that God was transforming a warrior into a king. Kings belong in palaces with all the finery and pomp and circumstance of a good upbringing and a rich lineage. That's not always so when God is the event planner of the coronation ceremony. David's equipping process and that of the men that were entrusted in his charge began at the Cave of Adullam. Let's revisit 1 Samuel 22:1 and 2 as we take an inside look at this man cave that we have since learned was literally, a center for life development, not just for David, but for the lives of thousands who would eventually come and be impacted and follow him. Just as many lives were changed, birthed out of these four hundred men that later grew to six hundred. Great things happened as a result of this encounter.

> *"So David departed from there and escaped to the Cave of Adullam and when his brothers and all his father's house heard of it they went down there to him, everyone who was in distress and everyone who was in debt and everyone who was discontented gathered to him and he became captain over them and there were about 400 men with him."*

David's man cave was a destitute location, neighborhood, and environment, whichever noun you want to use to describe his dark surroundings. Caves during that time did not have electricity. They did not have running water. They did not have restroom facilities. They were places that the who's who did not go to live in. The affluent would have never chosen this place to live. They were filled with insects, snakes, bats, scorpions and all other types of venomous and deadly insects and reptiles that were in that particular region. Especially during times when it was raining or there was increment weather and all these various type of creatures were seeking shelter. They would find it in these cave-like environments.

anointing
verb (used with object)
1. to rub or sprinkle on; apply an unguent, ointment, or oily liquid to.
2. to smear with any liquid.

3. to consecrate or make sacred in a ceremony that includes the token applying of oil: He anointed the new high priest.
4. to dedicate to the service of God.[5]

Keep in mind in 1Samuel 16, David was anointed as the future king of Israel. So many with David's anointing as the future leader of Israel and his position in Saul's administration as the general over Saul's entire army would have felt entitled to live an affluent life. It's rare that you find people who have risen to a place where David was without a societal expectation for them to live a comfortable life, in an affluent neighborhood, driving expensive cars and wearing tailored clothes. It's just what society expected. There was a huge gap between the "haves and the have nots." At his level, we would have expected David to be living somewhere else enjoying the good things in life.

However David made himself content in his destitute cave neighborhood for this season in his life. Most people would have never believed David was living under God's anointing. If we were to ask 1,000 believers today if someone was living in David's man cave environment was under God's anointing, many modern day believers, in the midst of all of this prosperity foolishness going on, would have said no. Why? Because God's anointing is often associated with status and an affluent lifestyle. David's destitute living situation is often associated with failure and defeat. So clearly most people back then and also today would not have associated God's anointing being upon David's life. But let me make this crystal clear that David even in the

5   http://dictionary.reference.com/browse/anoint?s=t

midst of his living in his destitute situation was clearly God's anointed one. Romans 11:29 says *"for the gifts and the calling of God are irrevocable."*

He was anointed by God, but he did not live, in the best neighborhood. He was anointed by God, but he wasn't driving the biggest car. He was anointed by God and didn't have the finest of clothes. He was anointed by God and was living as a fugitive. Don't determine someone's anointing by their status or address because like David your anointing might lead you to a season of living in a destitute situation. You better not get it twisted, there are a whole lot of anointed people living in poverty stricken conditions. Now they may not stay there forever, but at the end of the day, believe that the anointing is not just exclusively for those who live in middle-class and rich neighborhoods. God's anointing doesn't care what your address is. God's anointing can go wherever he wants it to.

God's anointing is upon his people and it doesn't matter whether or not his people stay in an apartment where there are drugs everywhere, where there are rats and roaches and ants everywhere. Nobody's doing exterminating. God's anointing for his people rests there as well as it rests in a 16,000 square foot house with gold toilets and faucets. You better recognize that God's anointing is a gift for his people that is not based on status and location and so don't you dare think that because somebody makes more money than you that they have more of God's anointing than you do. We play that kind of foolishness today. All the stuff that surrounds pastors in a church setting is temporary. I hope you know that the pulpit is temporary. All the walls, the chairs, the big building—all the stuff that surrounds my life is temporary. When people see the stuff, I usually have an abundance of people asking about how I'm living under God's anointing.

People may think that I'm so anointed now, but they really don't understand the word of God. God anointed me back when I got saved. God's anointing is just as powerful on me today as it was back then. God's anointing comes with the Holy Spirit and the empowerment to do what he's called us to do. If you think God's anointing is on me more now than you are sadly mistaken. I may have grown spiritually. I may have gotten wiser. Those things may be different about me now but God's anointing was just as much on me back then as it is now.

Don't somehow equate my spiritual anointing to the physical possessions that are around me. I'm not more anointed now than I was back then. That's crazy and don't you dare look at me and then look at somebody who is pastoring 100 folk and somehow think that I'm more anointed than they are. God's anointing was on David and he was living in a cave. No running water. No lights. No bathroom facilities. None of that and God's anointing was all over that man of God. Like David, your destitute living conditions can be God's appointed season of growth for you and not be about a lack of faith. Walking in God's anointing is not limited to your geographical location or the season of life you may find yourself in. Move forward in faith and embrace your God assignment wherever He has you. You are an anointed man of God, so do what David did and be content in the season you may find yourself in. The one thing about seasons that have been evident since the beginning of time is that eventually they are going to change. Nothings ever remains the same except God and His anointing.

ANSWER ME WHEN I CALL ...

The cave had begun to grow on him. He'd lived in the palace and slept in pastures but coming back to this cave after a brutal battle was somewhat comforting to him. It was now his home and that of many others. This is the place that God met him when he began this journey. It is in this unconventional place that He counsels and strengthens him. The Cave of Adullam, with its bats and rats had become a place of refuge and relief to this tired warrior's heart. He knew if God was with him, he could endure anything.

Psalm 4
Answer me when I call, O God of my righteousness!
You have relieved me in my distress;
Be gracious to me and hear my prayer.

O sons of men, how long will my honor become a reproach?
How long will you love what is worthless and aim at
deception? Selah.

But know that the LORD has set apart the godly man for
Himself;
The LORD hears when I call to Him.

Tremble, and do not sin;
Meditate in your heart upon your bed, and be still. Selah.

Offer the sacrifices of righteousness,
And trust in the LORD.

Many are saying, "Who will show us any good?"
Lift up the light of Your countenance upon us, O LORD!

You have put gladness in my heart,
More than when their grain and new wine abound.

In peace I will both lie down and sleep,
For You alone, O LORD, make me to dwell in safety.

CHAPTER SIX

THE MAN CAVE
POSTURE OF RELIEF

relief

noun

1. a feeling of reassurance and relaxation following release from anxiety or distress.

   "much to her relief, she saw the door open" [6]

he relief that we are discussing in this chapter is not the kind that you see in a Rolaids commercial. It is the kind of relief that comes when you are going through a season of trials and tribulations and you are offered a divine rest in the midst of it all. Let's revisit David and his men in the cave of Adullam. The word Adullam means sealed off place and the cave of Adullam became a place of relief during a very harsh

6   http://transitionalmeltdown.com/2014/04/21/r-is-for-relief/

season in David's life. From the outside looking in it appeared that he was down for the count, but in the supernatural God was conducting his own life development training for David. Others may mistake this season as evidence of your lack of faith and say, "You are here because you just don't have faith." That's crazy. If somebody ever tells you that just tell them that they're Biblically illiterate.

There are so many men and women of God, from Joseph until the apostles who were misunderstood and persecuted for all the wrong reasons but in the book of books, they are recorded as great people of faith. Some of the prophets in the Old Testament suffered horrendous attacks upon their bodies and were ostracized from civilization. In the New Testament, John the Baptist had his head cut off, Jesus was crucified, and the apostles were murdered because of their beliefs. See we've got to realize that what a person may be experiencing is just for a temporary season in their lives like David. If it's not, Paul said, *"For to me, to live is Christ and to die is gain."* It is well with my soul, either way.

So your condition may be temporary, just a season, in God's center for life development. You may be in a touchy situation right now. God's just developing character in you that's going to serve as a launching pad to elevate you in the presence of your doubters and your haters. What often times gets us upset is not that we're destitute but because sometimes when we're going through tough times our doubters and haters put us there. They think they put us there and they want us to stay there and they believe we're never going to get out. It's very frustrating but if we remain faithful and trust Him and walk with Him, God will deliver us.

David knew from personal experience how God can elevate you in the midst of a storm to the shock of your enemies. The Psalms are full of examples of how God caused him to triumph over his enemies.

In the midst of your enemies God can suddenly perform a miracle and raise you up right in the front of them. God showed up for the Prophet Elijah in front of 450 Prophets of Baal and an audience. God not only showed them He was the one and only God, but He also gave his man of God dominion over them. Each and every one of them were slaughtered there that day.

So for all of those who don't believe that you have a God purpose and you are called by Him because of your temporary season, just wait. Remain faithful and one day God will elevate you right in the presence of your doubters and your haters. God can do whatever he wants to do with his anointed chosen people. He doesn't need my permission, nor does he have to get the permission of my doubters and my haters. He can do whatever He wants to do. So David's man cave was a destitute location but that did not stop him from fulfilling his God purpose to equip and train up an army of men to the glory of God.

David's man cave was also a place of relief. Sometimes in the midst of these trying times we need some relief. We need a place of refuge. Remember the word Adullam means a shielded off place and the cave of Adullam became a place of relief and refuge for David and his men.

David later identifies the God behind the relief or the refuge he experienced in places like the cave of Adullam when he wrote Psalms 91:1–4. In David's mind he had to have the cave of Adullam as one of those places where he found relief while he was being pursued by the insane, paranoid, murdering Saul. If this Psalm doesn't get you excited I don't know which one will. God is something else. All these promises in the Bible and you're worrying about whether or not He can pay your $60 light bill. Why would you be worried about the light bill and you serve this kind of God?

> Psalm 91:4 states, "He who dwells in the shelter of the most high will abide in the shadow of the All Mighty. I will say to the Lord my refuge and my fortress, my God in whom I trust for it is He who delivers you from the snare of the trapper and from the deadly pestilence. He will cover you with pinions and that's a form of wings and under His wings you may seek refuge. His faithfulness is a shield in bulwarks."

A bulwark is a fortress or wall that is set up for protection. Here God is letting us know through David that He can provide relief and refuge in the midst of any storm you're going through. This is the God that is behind you.

David's man cave was a place of relief and it was a refuge. Notice how the God of relief and refuge in Psalms 91 used the cave of Adullam as part of his plan to provide a sanctuary, for David. Do you know that the God of all the universe can literally come Himself and just physically cover us and provide relief or refuge for us? For instance, when Daniel was in the lion's den God had to come Himself and do something out of the ordinary, miraculous and somehow keep him safe from ravenous lions. God stepped in then, but that's not how he does it most of the time. Most of the time God uses things like the caves of Adullam when you're going through the storms of life to be that place that provides relief and refuge for you. While you're praying, asking God to send you relief, He may be saying I've already sent it to you.

I already provided you with a cave of Adullam, but you don't want to go. You're going to the wrong cave when you're going through the tough times and you think the cave of Adullam looks like a night club. Or you may think it looks like a bar and you just go and try to drink away your problems. You're in the wrong place. Perhaps you think it's at your secret lover's house, Sampson did and we all know what happened to him. You're at the wrong cave. You've got to find the right cave in order to get your relief. Some people say, well I'm going to find it in a university. I'm going to go to school. I'm going to get educated. I'm going to get relief and it's going to soothe and satisfy my soul. It's the wrong place. You're not going to find that place at your job. You're not going to find it in your refrigerator in the meat and potatoes. That's not where you're going to find it. You're at the wrong cave.

God uses caves of Adullam like our local churches for relief during the storm. Most churches have groups that come together on a regular basis such as men's ministries, women's ministries, prayer groups, and they meet together to pray. They have Bible study and Sunday services where you get an opportunity to fellowship with other believers. God has many caves of Adullam right within the walls of your local church. You've been asking God for some relief, but you don't want to come to the cave of Adullam. You run to the arms of your Delilah when you should be running to God. You want to sit in front of your television and forget about your problems as you watch *Crisis* and somehow you think this will solve your problems. Come on! We've got to find our personal caves of Adullam if we want to find some relief.

Your local church has many of them. You want a place of refuge and relief, start getting more active. Start becoming a part of a group of people who want some of the same things you want. They want their families to be successful. They want to stay married. They want a husband or a wife to love them. They want children to obey them. I can promise you, if you say, "I'm kind of like David right now, my season of desperation and despair has not ended," and you seek relief and refuge in those other places, you're not going to find it.

Some of us love sports, especially local sports and you may say, "Oh I just love a good old high school football game." You can go all you want. Your team can win state. You can jump up and down, do cart wheels and wear their jersey. You can do all of that and after they win state and you're driving home I promise you the enemy's going to say "Hello. You thought I was gone didn't you? You thought because you were acting a fool at the game going crazy, you thought because you were screaming, hollering that somehow you blocked me out. You thought I was gone!" If the problem's at the house, as soon as you see the house, the enemy is going to say "I'm waiting for you right behind that door." The enemy is waiting for you because you didn't do anything to spiritually strengthen yourself for the battle. You're going right back into the same situation with less energy to deal with what's facing you.

David's man cave was open to anyone who was seeking relief and refuge. If they had the courage to make the journey, God met them there and provided His comforting arm to strengthen them for the rest of their season. Where is your cave of Adullam? Has it brought you the relief that God promises in Psalm 91? If not, try your local church; they specialize in rejects, misfits, and the misunderstood.

SIR, REMEMBER ME ...

David could see the light at the end of the proverbial tunnel, he was on his way to Hebron soon. His men had become faithful devoted warriors. He thanked God daily for their loyalty. He would put them up against any king's army including Saul's. To date, his former king had never been able to capture them. Thank God.

One of the new recruits came to the door of his tent and asked permission to enter. He acknowledged him and granted him access. He approached David rather sheepishly. He beckoned him to come closer. David said to him, "Speak." He immediately fell on his face and said, "Sir, Remember me when you come in your kingdom?"

Over 1000 years later ...

The Crucifixion
When they came to the place called The Skull, there they crucified Him and the criminals, one on the right and the other on the left. But Jesus was saying, "Father, forgive them;

for they do not know what they are doing." And they cast lots, dividing up His garments among themselves. And the people stood by, looking on. And even the rulers were sneering at Him, saying, "He saved others; let Him save Himself if this is the Christ of God, His Chosen One. "The soldiers also mocked Him, coming up to Him, offering Him sour wine, and saying, "If You are the King of the Jews, save Yourself!" Now there was also an inscription above Him, "THIS IS THE KING OF THE JEWS."One of the criminals who were hanged there was hurling abuse at Him, saying, "Are You not the Christ? Save Yourself and us!" But the other answered, and rebuking him said, "Do you not even fear God, since you are under the same sentence of condemnation? And we indeed are suffering justly, for we are receiving what we deserve for our deeds; but this man has done nothing wrong." And he was saying, "Jesus, remember me when You come in Your kingdom!" And He said to him, "Truly I say to you, today you shall be with Me in Paradise."

CHAPTER SEVEN

THE MAN CAVE POSTURE OF LOYALTY

loyalty

noun

1. the state or quality of being loyal; faithfulness to commitments or obligations.

2. faithful adherence to a sovereign, government, leader, cause, etc.

3. an example or instance of faithfulness, adherence, or the like: a man with fierce loyalties.[7]

Let's take a further look inside of David's man cave. We've learned thus far that it was transformed into a center for life development. Not just for him, but for those that he was leading. I want to talk about David's man

---

7   http://dictionary.reference.com/browse/loyalties

cave from the perspective of some of the things we can learn about relationships. I want to begin with the fact that David's man cave solidified his loyalty to his friends. We know from 1 Samuel's account of David's time in the cave of Adullam that he became their captain, but he also became a very loyal friend.

David's experience with his men in very harsh places like the cave of Adullam literally served to solidify his loyalty to his friends. David proved his loyalty to his friends after Saul's death when he moved to Judah with his men and was made King.

Now in 2nd Samuel 2:3 the Bible says: *"And David brought up his men who were with him, each with his household and they lived in the city of Hebron,"* which primarily was in the hill country of Judah. Now, for the first time in 10 long years, David was no longer a fugitive and those men who once suffered with him were now invited to reign with him. So David didn't kick his men to the curb. During the time when David was struggling, didn't have nice places to stay, and he was a fugitive, these men followed him. They fought along with him and bled with him. They were hungry with him, were cold with him, and went through the same struggles that he did. When David was reappointed – particularly at this time, he was just King over Judah. When he had risen to where God anointed him to be, he did not kick his friends to the curb. The bible is clear that he was devoted to them for their sacrifice. Not only did he bring his men with him, but each of their households were invited to reign with David, as well.

Something happened in the harsh places like the cave of Adullam that helped solidify David's commitment to loyalty. During those hard times, David grew and he developed as a man and something happened there that taught him the importance of being loyal.

I want you to realize that there is something valuable in being a loyal friend, a loyal son, a loyal daughter, a loyal student, a loyal employee. When success comes our way, we should be loyal to our friends that we made in the trenches. Don't trade them in for a newer model when your status changes. Sometimes we develop selective amnesia when we reach a certain socio-economic status in life and we forget those who were in the trenches with us. David wasn't like that, he remembered his friends.

Loyalty is losing its luster in today's world. It used to be something that people yearned for and longed to do. But in today's world loyalty is an old fashioned notion because change has become more important than commitment. People often are not loyal, but they will change a friend, they will change a situation in a heartbeat without considering the value of a long-term relationship. We've been trained to be people of change. If you look at most commercials, most commercials are asking you to change. They're asking you to change your car. They're asking you to change your house. They're asking you to change from Skippy to Jiffy. They're asking you to change and we do it because we have been sold on the concept that the grass is greener on the other side. As God's people, we have to remember that we are not of this world. God requires us, like He required David to have a basic fundamental commitment to loyalty.

God's conduits that he uses to help us – like family, like friends, like churches, like other institutions – should be the first to share in our accomplishments. But they are often forgotten and become footnotes in our lives. Sometimes those very people who help us to get to where we are become insignificant once we reach our goals and fulfill our desires.

For example, mothers and fathers, play such a vital part in you getting to where you are today. There are so many elderly parents that have kids that have good jobs; that are making good money and living in nice houses and their mother can't even pay her light bill. Where is your loyalty? Would you let one of your BFF's (Best Female Friend's) light bill come due? What if one of your fraternity brothers or sorority sisters have a need of that nature? You'll run across town to pay that bill. But your own mother can't depend on you. She was there when your nose was snotty and runny; when you went to the bathroom all over yourself. Who stayed up with you when you were sick and you can't even pay her light bill. Shame on you. Where is your loyalty?

One of the things that I'm so glad to know is that there are pastors out there who have a Davidic mindset when it comes to developing people. They have been loyal to the Lord in keeping the ministry about the people. They try to make sure that everyone sitting in their pews understand their ministry is about the people. At Fallbrook, we don't have designated parking or seating for our ministers, ministerial staff, or VIP preachers because we are a people centered church.

You can go to Macy's and they will have their employees park four blocks away and you'll come to church and half the parking is reserved for the head of the usher board, head of the deacon's board, head of the bishops board, and the head of the pastor's board. You got all kinds of reserved parking spots. It ought to be about the people.

David was loyal to his friends. I believe that's the reason why God has elevated churches with Davidic mindsets to be beacons of transformation in our city. Our church is a prime example. We shouldn't be where we are today. The bottom line is when you look at the numbers and at our size, it was virtually impossible to do what we do. We recently started a building project—with the expectation that God would bring an increase in the size of our congregation because the people here are committed and loyal to keeping our ministry about the people.

Loyalty is essential. Family, friends, churches and organizations that have stood with us, they deserve more than verbal loyalty. They deserve loyalty in action. It's easy to say that you're loyal, and I'm a loyal friend. It's another thing to be one. Sometimes when we talk about loyalty, we may say, 'I love my mother!' Well, do you really love her? How often do you go see her? Well, if you love her, then prove it by being loyal.

I can't say that I love my family, but I'm not loyal to my family. Taking care of everybody else but not taking care of those in my own home is dangerous. The Bible says that a man that doesn't take care of his own family is worse than an unbeliever. We ought to have a sense of loyalty towards those who are in our own households and in the household of faith. And those places and people and organizations that stood with us, they deserve more than just verbal loyalty. They deserve loyalty in action. We do that when we share our time and our resources with them.

You'll see some individual's resumes and they'll say, 'I'm a member of Phi Beta Summa Cum Laude, Chapter Seven of 9542 subsection. They've got a resume full of civic and social positions, but then if you dig a little bit deeper you may find out the last time they went to a meeting was in 1999. If that is so, you ought to turn your membership card in because you're not loyal. You're not faithful to the organization's mission and purpose. If you say you're a member of something and you hadn't been there for 15 years, you haven't given a dime, you haven't supported it, you ought to take your card and drop it in the fireplace because that's about as much as it means. It means nothing because you're not proving your loyalty.

My nephew, when he graduated from the University of Pennsylvania (it is an Ivy League School), I went to his commencement. They have lots of money coming in through various endowments and alumni who are committed to that school. When he graduated, one of the last things the president told each member of his graduating class was that he expected their continued loyalty and he expected them to give back to the institution that invested in them. Even though they were paying for tuition, he expected them to give back.

Sometimes church folk will give more to their alma mater than they give to the church of the Lord Jesus Christ. Every member should do what God has called them to do in regards to the tithe. Take a moment and ask yourselves if you are allocating not just your money, but also your time and your resources to forward God's kingdom through your local church? Would God consider you a loyal member at your place of worship? Or would your attendance just be a footnote on your

Franklin Calendar? How will the church rank when it comes to your family and those who are important to you? Are they just a footnote or are they are part of your commitment to loyalty?

We've got to start talking about loyalty. We've got to start talking about how we say "I love you and I'm committed to you," but then we don't show it. The proof is in the pudding. David was loyal to those men. He left us an example and we must be loyal, as well.

When David made it back on top, all of the warriors who stood by him and helped him get to the top again, David said, 'I'm not kicking y'all to the curb and start running with all these city upscale kind of folk. I'm rolling with these former vagabonds. They're going to make up my circle that I'm going to surround myself with. You know why folks make mistakes sometimes when they become a high roller, shot caller and all that kind of stuff? When they become a high roller with some prestige, they surround themselves with nothing but new folk. It's the biggest mistake that you can make because you don't know the motive of all the new folks. The new folks may just be getting with you because you are a high roller, but let you stop rolling and see how fast they get out of Dodge.

And if you think being a high roller status is forever, I've got news for you. You must not watch the news. Joe Paterno was at Penn State over 60 years, where he coached for over 46 years and they let him go with a phone call. I totally agree with how the university handled this matter based on the circumstances, but Joe was without a job before you could blink an eye. The next time you think you're that important remember that all it took was a telephone call saying, 'Hey, Joe. Don't come back.'

Loyalty – is so, so, so crucial. Be loyal to your friends, family and the entities that have been loyal to you. David did and it solidified his journey to possess his kingdom.

SOMETIMES IT TAKES
A GOOD WOMAN!

*David's captains were teasing him about the beautiful woman who stopped him from shedding the blood of innocent people because she was married to a fool. They'd recently heard that her husband fell over dead at a festival. The question on the table was, 'Did David stop **dead** in his tracks because of her beauty or was it because she was a woman of discernment?' The king ended the conversation with this statement. 'She's both; therefore I would be a bigger fool if I didn't marry her.'*

Abigail Intercedes

But one of the young men told Abigail, Nabal's wife, saying, "Behold, David sent messengers from the wilderness to greet our master, and he scorned them. Yet the men were very good to us, and we were not insulted, nor did we miss anything as long as we went about with them, while we were in the fields.

They were a wall to us both by night and by day, all the time we were with them tending the sheep. Now therefore, know and consider what you should do, for evil is plotted against our master and against all his household; and he is such a worthless man that no one can speak to him."

Then Abigail hurried and took two hundred loaves of bread and two jugs of wine and five sheep already prepared and five measures of roasted grain and a hundred clusters of raisins and two hundred cakes of figs, and loaded them on donkeys. She said to her young men, "Go on before me; behold, I am coming after you." But she did not tell her husband Nabal. It came about as she was riding on her donkey and coming down by the hidden part of the mountain, that behold, David and his men were coming down toward her; so she met them. Now David had said, "Surely in vain I have guarded all that this man has in the wilderness, so that nothing was missed of all that belonged to him; and he has returned me evil for good. May God do so to the enemies of David, and more also, if by morning I leave as much as one male of any who belong to him."

When Abigail saw David, she hurried and dismounted from her donkey, and fell on her face before David and bowed herself to the ground. ²⁴ *She fell at his feet and said, "On me alone, my lord, be the blame. And please let your maidservant speak to you, and listen to the words of your maidservant. Please do not let my lord pay attention to this worthless man, Nabal, for as his name is, so is he. Nabal is his name and folly is with him; but I your maidservant did not see the young men of my lord whom you sent.*

"Now therefore, my lord, as the LORD LIVES, AND AS YOUR SOUL LIVES, SINCE THE LORD HAS RESTRAINED YOU FROM SHEDDING BLOOD, AND FROM AVENGING YOURSELF BY YOUR OWN HAND, NOW THEN LET YOUR ENEMIES AND THOSE WHO SEEK EVIL AGAINST MY LORD, BE AS NABAL. *Now let this gift which your maidservant has brought to my lord be given to the young men who accompany my lord. Please forgive the transgression of your maidservant; for the* LORD WILL CERTAINLY MAKE FOR MY LORD AN ENDURING HOUSE, BECAUSE MY LORD IS FIGHTING THE BATTLES OF THE LORD, AND EVIL WILL NOT BE FOUND IN YOU ALL YOUR DAYS. *Should anyone rise up to pursue you and to seek your life, then the life of my lord shall be bound in the bundle of the living with the* LORD YOUR GOD; BUT THE LIVES OF YOUR ENEMIES HE WILL SLING OUT AS FROM THE HOLLOW OF A SLING. *And when the* LORD DOES FOR MY LORD ACCORDING TO ALL THE GOOD THAT HE HAS SPOKEN CONCERNING YOU, AND APPOINTS YOU RULER OVER ISRAEL, *this will not cause grief or a troubled heart to my lord, both by having shed blood without cause and by my lord having avenged himself. When the* LORD DEALS WELL WITH MY LORD, THEN REMEMBER YOUR MAIDSERVANT. *"*

THEN DAVID SAID TO ABIGAIL, "BLESSED BE THE LORD GOD OF ISRAEL, WHO SENT YOU THIS DAY TO MEET ME, *and blessed be your discernment, and blessed be you, who have kept me this day from bloodshed and from avenging myself by my own hand. Nevertheless, as the* LORD GOD OF ISRAEL LIVES, WHO HAS RESTRAINED ME FROM HARMING YOU, UNLESS YOU HAD COME QUICKLY TO MEET ME, SURELY THERE WOULD NOT HAVE BEEN LEFT

TO NABAL UNTIL THE MORNING LIGHT AS MUCH AS ONE MALE." So David received from her hand what she had brought him and said to her, "Go up to your house in peace. See, I have listened to you and granted your request." (1Samuel:18 – 35)

CHAPTER EIGHT

THE MAN CAVE POSTURE OF DISCERNMENT

discernment

noun

the ability to see and understand people, things, or stituations clearly and intelligently[8]

avid's man cave certified the veracity of his friends. That's a big word that says that it certified that they were real or true friends. You see, David was blessed to make friends in the trenches. The best place to make friends is when you're on the bottom. If you say you want to make lifelong friends, the best time to make lifelong friends is when things are not going right.

---

8   http://www.merriam-webster.com/dictionary/discernment

David was blessed to make friends in the trenches because, he was able to certify their friendship as genuine. David's man cave turned out to be a great way to certify the veracity, the authenticity of his friends before he gained the throne.

So that means that some of you if you're planning on rising to "king" status, I suggest that you now begin to surround yourself with friends that you can trust. When you don't have anything, and nobody knows you, nobody likes you, those people who are around you now, they're around you because they may really care about you. But let you get a little money, and you will begin to see relatives that you didn't know you had. Some of you know exactly what I'm talking about. You get a raise and watch how your new found friends are going to start hovering around you.

I've seen some of my buddies back home get McDonald's jobs back when I was in high school and find friends. I'm talking about they were making $3.35 an hour. As soon as they got the job, dudes would hang around them. You know why? Because they knew that when Friday or the weekend comes, they got somebody working that can finance their weekend partying habits.

So if somebody's going to be your boy with a job like that, you better not start making a six or seven figure income. Imagine, everybody would want to be your friend. You better not mess around and hit that lotto. They're going to start coming out of the woodworks.

According to an article in New York Times titled *A Financial Plan for Misbehaving Lottery Winners* by Carl Richards, "On average, 90 percent of lottery winners go through their winnings in five years or less." One of the reasons this is true is because of those friends and long lost relatives that show up with their hands out and sob stories. 'Ah, man, you know we were always boys,' and all that kind of stuff. And he would steal your lunch money every day when you were in school. But, 'You know you were always my boy!'

Proverbs 17:17 says: *A friend loves at all times.* You want to get a good friend? Find one that loves you at all times. You know when you watch the news and they do an expose' on someone famous, you can figure out who their friends are real, real fast. These are the ones that come to the courtroom every day of the trial and sob when the sentence is read.

One of the most disappointing things that I've seen in my life was Bernie Madoff. One of Bernie Madoff's son's did a news interview about his father. Now, I'm not condoning what Bernie Madoff did. Bernie Madoff was a crook. But he had two sons. One is still alive. Now, they don't have to necessarily agree with his conduct, but it's never acceptable in the eyes of God for you to go on public TV and talk about your father the way that he did.

In fact, those close friends and family members who were around the Madoffs say Bernie Madoff was a good father to his children when they were growing up. Some of you might disagree with me, but let me explain this. You may be thinking, "Bernie Madoff stole all that money, he isn't nothing but a crook and he's going to burn in Hell!" Well, in the eyes of God, somebody stealing something small is still stealing. Bernie Madoff's stealing billions of dollars was just a more complex scam. Stealing is stealing in the eyes of God. Perhaps when you were young, you stole for your neighborhood convenience store. Especially if your peers were doing it, you were stealing everything you could get your hands on and God still loves you and saved you. God is not a respecter of persons, He can save Bernie Madoff.

If you're making a mistake means that your friends cut you off, then they probably weren't very good friends in the first place. Proverbs 17:17 says *"A friend loves at all times and a brother is born for adversity."* Adversity is a great filtering process to identify genuine friends. If you lose your job, take notice of who is still making themselves available to you. Especially if you're the one that's always paying for something. Adversity will get rid of those who really don't like you.

Sometimes if you make it to the top you might need to tell those people who have been following you, just to test them, that the well has run dry. Just take all your money and put it somewhere else so you won't be telling a fib and say, 'Man, all my money just kind of went somewhere else.' And they're going to ask you this question, 'You ain't got no more money?' 'No, I don't have any more money in this account.' 'That account's dry.' 'Hold on. Hold on. Time out. You don't have no more money?' Before you get the words out of your mouth, they'll be halfway down the street trying to catch up with their next mark.

Brothers, I want to let you know that there is such a thing as a gold digger. You know, you can have a dude that's a gold digger, and you can have a lady that's a gold digger. She's digging for gold. She's on an exploratory mission to find a brother with some gold.

The way you fix that is to keep your financial status quiet when you initially meet someone and you are trying to develop a relationship with them. If you're trying to find real, genuine love, you don't want to let her know you're wealthy. Otherwise, you're going to be attracting a whole lot of ladies when they find out that your account is large. What you may want to do to test if this is real love, just take her to a Taco Bell. Run for the border. Sit down and start eating and observe her response. If she eats the taco like its filet mignon then you can say, 'Hey, I got me a good one!' Now, if she looks at that taco like, 'I can't believe you took me to Taco Bell. I don't eat tacos.' This young lady may be looking to be financed and not romanced. When she is spending her own money, she'll not think twice about *running for the border*. Obviously she's not the woman for you.

When Lebron James built his inner circle, he included some lifelong friends. Some people questioned his wisdom. But what they did not consider in their intellectual probe was the loyalty quotient. James choose wisely. The guys that he has around him, are intelligent young brothers who have already proved that they were in his corner. The news media was making all kinds of negative comments about his decision and I didn't understand that. If he believed that those were his lifelong friends and he knows that he's going to make millions of dollars as a result of his athletic ability, why not include some of his friends to enjoy this wealth that he has? His good friend Rich Paul is now handling his playing contracts, in addition to being a part of the founders of the marketing company LRMR, which was formed by childhood friends Paul, Maverick Carter and Randy Mims. The company adopted the first letter of the first name of the four friends. It's working which some consider rare, but when you form relationships based on having a genuine interest in the overall success of others, it can do nothing but bring positive results. David knew that and implemented that philosophy in the man cave.

Now, I'm not condoning what some of the other athletes do when they've experienced a level of success. Hiring friends that are living lives that are out of control and doing crazy stuff around them. I'm talking about some of your friends that have proven their sincerity and are good people who have dreams that you can help come true. What's wrong with that? We do know that (particularly in the 70's) black athletes have signed some of the worst deals in American history in all areas of sports. Do you know who the people were that were taking all their money? Dudes in suits. It wasn't gang bangers, crack heads, or the dudes from the neighborhood. These fellows would sit them down and make them sign contracts that were absolutely crazy.

Do you know how many fighters that boxed in the 70's that don't have a dime today? Why? Because their promoters got most of the money. And so at the end of the day, these lawyers and predators, when they see somebody getting ready to make a whole lot of money, they come in thinking in the back of their mind, 'I'm getting ready to get paid.' So Lebron was using wisdom in selecting his trusted friends who were qualified to run his organization,

The number one way to get a job in America is through networking, which is the business way of saying, old-school hookup. If I was to take a bus and was able to get all of us on the bus and just drive up the street to every small business, almost everybody that's working in those small businesses got their job because of somebody they knew; a relative, a cousin, a next door neighbor. I would ask those who questioned Lebron's decision, what's wrong with him hiring some trusted loyal friends to work alongside him while he continues to build his company and career? We ought to be committed to being loyal. He found out whom he could trust and he put some of those around him. He used discernment in selecting his staff.

Age is not a factor in God's kingdom when it comes to success. Some of you may be real young, but you are going to be great ambassadors for God. I know some of you are going to make it to extremely high places. Can you please remember this? When you get there, don't forget everybody who helped get you to where you are. Don't let them be a footnote in your wonderful life. Use discernment in your selection process, but don't turn your life over to people who say they will have your best interest at heart just because they work for someone else or have a degree. Try the spirit. They should have to earn the right to be your manager, lawyer, banker, or producer.

Next, David's man cave verified the mendacity of his enemies before he gained his kingship. That's just another one of those big words. That just means that he verified who the phonies were that were attempting to influence his life. Places like the cave of Adullam and the Forest of Hereth helped David verify who his enemies were like Doeg.

Look at verse 1 Samuel 22:22, *Then David said to Abiathar, "I knew on that day when Doeg the Edomite was there, that he would surely tell Saul."* Doeg is working for

Saul; he's his head shepherd. Doeg, for some reason, is in the City of Nob, which is a holy city where the priests reside. So, basically, Doeg is spending time with the Lord. He's at church. David needs some food so he goes to the Holy City and he goes to see Ahimelech, the Chief Priest, and he asked him for some food.

Now, David is running from Saul. Saul's trying to kill him. David knew who Doeg was because the verse we just read said that he knew him.

Here's the scenario. David's coming, running from Saul. He comes into the city, he comes into where the Chief Priest was. Doeg had to be somewhere in that sanctuary and so he sees Doeg and probably said, 'Hey, what's up?' Because, remember, they knew each other. Doeg probably said, 'What's up, Dave?' But, David because he was streetwise, had an inkling that Doeg's loyalty was to Saul. He made a mental note in his mind thinking, 'Man! Why did Doeg have to see me? Because I know, he is going to drop a dime on me. I know he's going to squeal on me. I know he's going to do it.'

Exactly what David thought was going to happen, happened. Doeg dropped the dime on him, trying to elevate his status in the eyes of the king. The moral of this story is, don't ever get to the point where you're naïve about people and their capability for betrayal. Some of you may be thinking today, 'Everybody likes me.' Yet Jesus was the sinless, holy son of God; never cursed, swear, lied, cheated or anything. He was the perfect son of God and there was a lot of people who hated Jesus. If you believe that there is no one who doesn't like you, you are out of your natural born mind.

Do you know one of the major reasons for this deception is our lack of maturity? We are so naïve to think that our world is untouchable when we face adversity every day.

When I was a kid growing up, we used to walk through certain neighborhoods where we didn't know people. I had a pretty large family on my mom's side and I have an older brother. So I was pretty protected. But there were areas in those neighborhoods where I didn't I have any protection. There were times when I would walk home or walk somewhere and I would see some dudes that looked like they were up to no good and I would take the longer way to where I needed to go. Why? Because, I had common sense. I see some dudes that look like they were up to no good, I'm not going that way.

You're a believer, you love God, but you're naïve about people. Don't put your antennas down. Where was Doeg when he saw David? He wasn't at the club. He wasn't at a frat party. He wasn't at a bar. Doeg was at the temple! So you know what that tells me? That tells me that the person sitting right next to you might be scheming on you. We're looking for them to be carrying pitchforks and all that kind of crazy stuff, but it's just not so.

Recently, we had helicopters buzzing all over the church. Harris County Sheriff's Department was rolling all through our parking lot. We were trying to take our kids to the playground they said, 'Don't go to the playground! Schools are locked down!' We asked them, 'What's going on?' We found out some kids were going through the neighborhood kicking doors in and stealing other people's stuff. They were not dressed like devils, but they were dressed just like normal kids dress today.

Don't be naïve, Just because they say, 'Yes, sir. No, sir,' does not mean that they are good kids. You better watch what's going on in your neighborhood! You may love your next door neighbors, but if their son or daughter is a thief, you better lock your garage.

I know a lot of young people whom I love. I talk to them, counsel with them, and went to basketball games to watch them play. But some of those kids I wouldn't leave in my house without me being there. That doesn't mean that I don't love them. That just means I need to watch them. At any given day, you may see me talking to somebody that looks like they just robbed seven banks. I really don't care. But, at the same time, I need to be conscious of what I'm doing because at any moment, anybody can flip on you. And I mean anybody. Just don't be naïve about this life you are trying to live.

David was not naïve. The spirit told him that Doeg was up to no good and David knew him. We've got to put up the same safeguards and be discerning about the people we let into our lives. We've got to allow life to teach us to be on top of our game; to be observant, to be watchful, and to not assume anything. If it's 110 degrees on a summer day and somebody comes in the church with a trench coat on, we need to know about that quickly. About a year ago we had some guys that came on our church campus and they looked like they were up to no good. Our police officers questioned them and noticed that they were carrying weapons. They were arrested and they are now in prison. To this day, we don't know why they choose to visit our church. They were on probation and they were carrying guns, which is a violation of their probation agreement. So they never said why they were here but it was evident that their intentions were probably not good. My point is that it was obvious that they meant to harm parishioners and staff, if we'd ignored the threat, we would have been naïve about their intent and no telling how many lives would have been lost that day.

Years ago when we were awarded our charter school, one of the TEA Board Members also offered this advice to me, "If the news media rolls up here with their cameras, they aren't coming to see you, they aren't coming here to worship. They're coming here because you have got a problem somewhere." So it is critical to vet everyone who becomes a part of our charter school. The news headlines are full of reports of how a teacher was caught sleeping with a student or selling drugs at local schools. We will do our due diligence in investigating the staff that serve our children so that we won't be the cause of any of those headlines. Just like it's critical for us, it's also likewise for you. Trust, but verify. Be discerning when selecting your friends. It's hard to identify covert enemies, who are faking it until they make it. If they can withstand a season in the Cave of Adullam, then they are true loyal friends. If they are phonies, the cave experience will verify their intent real fast.

STIMULATED PRAYER, FAITH, PRAISE

The Ark of the Covenant was finally coming back to Israel. Everyone was in a festive uproar about its arrival. King David was no longer in the Cave of Adullam, he was now king over all of Israel. He and his men had come a mighty long way from those days in David's man cave. As he reflected on all God had brought him through, his heart nearly burst with gratitude to Him for His faithfulness. He wept.

So David went and brought up the ark of God from the house of Obededom into the city of David with gladness.

And it was so, that when they that bare the ark of the LORD had gone six paces, he sacrificed oxen and fatlings.

And David danced before the LORD with all his might; and David was girded with a linen ephod.

So David and all the house of Israel brought up the ark of the LORD with shouting, and with the sound of the trumpet. (2 Samuel 6:12 -15)

CHAPTER NINE

THE MAN CAVE POSTURE OF PRAYER, FAITH AND PRAISE

S o far, our look inside David's man cave revealed that it was a center for life development. David and the men he was leading learned to live their lives as fugitives. But David's man cave was not just about life development. It was a center for spiritual development.

Let's take a look again at our core scriptures in 1 Samuel 22:1-2.

"So David departed from them and escaped to the cave of Adullam and when his brothers and all of his father's household heard of it they went down there to him. Everyone who was in distress and everyone who was in debt and everyone who was discontented gathered to him

and he became captain over them. Now there were about 400 men with him."

Our core scripture establishes the who, what, and when of our scenario. Psalm 57 explains David's spiritual posture in the midst of it all.

Be gracious to me, O God, be gracious to me, for my soul takes refuge in You; And in the shadow of Your wings I will take refuge until destruction passes by. I will cry to God Most High, to God who accomplishes all things for me. He will send from heaven and save me; He reproaches him who tramples upon me. Selah. God will send forth His lovingkindness and His truth. My soul is among lions; I must lie among those who breathe forth fire, even the sons of men, whose teeth are spears and arrows and their tongue a sharp sword. Be exalted above the heavens, O God; Let Your glory be above all the earth. They have prepared a net for my steps; my soul is bowed down; they dug a pit before me; they themselves have fallen into the midst of it. Selah. 7 My heart is steadfast, O God, my heart is steadfast; I will sing, yes, I will sing praises! Awake, my glory! Awake, harp and lyre! I will awaken the dawn. I will give thanks to You, O Lord, among the peoples; I will sing praises to You among the nations. For Your lovingkindness is great to the heavens and Your truth to the clouds. Be exalted above the heavens, O God; Let Your glory be above all the earth.

Psalm 57

Psalm 57 specifically speaks to the adverse situation that David was experiencing in the cave of Adullam. In these harsh places, the Lord was able to shape and refine him in the natural sense. That's what we talked about in the last few chapters. Now we will talk about how it was also used for spiritual life development, for David to grow stronger in the Lord. The fact that David composed Psalms 57 and 142 during his experience in the cave of Adullam uncovers the impact the cave had on his life. He is writing in the midst of all of his pain, turmoil and difficulty. David writes about where he is with God, what God means to him, and what he believes about the Lord.

Sometimes we look in a negative fashion at those difficult seasons in our lives. But I believe that in the midst of those harsh and difficult days we accomplish some of the greatest spiritual advancement in our lives. God is not afraid of difficult days, and we don't have to be, either.

In Psalm 57 we see how God used the cave of Adullam to stimulate David in three spiritual elements. First, God stimulated him to assume the posture of prayer. Second, God stimulated David's faith in Him. Third, God stimulated him to assume the posture of praise. Let's begin. In Psalm 57:1-2, notice David's request of the Lord. "Be gracious to me O God. Be gracious to me for my soul take refuge in you and in the shadow of your wings I'll take refuge until destruction passes by." He is opening with this prayer. The psalm reveals David is clearly communicating with God during his difficult days. Where David does turns in the midst of his trouble and pain? He opens a line of communication with God. The cave of Adullam had removed David from his most loyal and trusted friend and confidant, Jonathan, the son of Saul. He was the one who David went to often during his time of trouble, to share with his trustworthy friend what was on his heart.

David later learned to share his difficult days not with Jonathan, but with the Lord. We have to realize that often we turn to everybody except God. We tell everybody else about our troubles, but we don't share them with the Lord. God was able to make sure that David understood whom he ought to be communicating with in his times of trouble. How? He removed everybody that was important in his life. David had God and God alone to share with. As we mentioned in an earlier chapter, prayer is much bigger than just asking. Most Christians view prayer as asking and they really don't understand what prayer is really all about.

prayer

noun, often attributive

[9]1 a (1): an address (as a petition) to God or a god in word or thought <said a prayer for the success of the voyage> (2): a set order of words used in praying

B: an earnest request or wish

> *"Prayer is simply a two-way conversation between you and God."*
>
> Billy Graham

How would you feel about somebody who was continuously asking you for something? Prayer should be much more than

---

9   http://www.merriam-webster.com/dictionary/prayer

that to you. It's not a one dimensional conversation. For David, prayer was sharing his entire life with God. You can't read the Psalms and not see that he was continuously pouring out his heart to God. In the life of the believer, prayer must rise above just asking. Are we able to ask? Yes, but it is so much more than that. You know how many times people go through troubled times and they're always looking for somebody that they can sit down and cry with and pour out their heart. We are always looking for a human being to do that with.

God brought David to a place to where all David could do was pour out his heart to God and we've got to learn from that because just like we cry in front of people, we ought to be crying on our knees before God. We ought to be sharing our lives with God, on a daily basis. Who are you sharing your life with? Some say I'm sharing my life with my husband. I'm sharing my life with my wife. I'm sharing my life with my mother. I'm sharing my life with my daddy. That's good, but sharing your life with God is so much better. We ought to be sharing our lives with God first. The first person you ought to run to when you get your promotion is not your husband, your wife, your daddy, your mother, your sister, or your brother. You ought to run to God, give him praise, and thank Him. Everybody else is secondary.

You know the reason why most people don't pray? They don't pray because they don't understand prayer. Prayer is not a formality, something we do because we have to. It is something we do because we want to communicate with our creator. In fact, I believe most believers pray more often than they think because prayer is communicating and sharing with God.

That means you're having a conversation with God. You're talking with God. You're saying, "Lord, Man, I'm having a messed up week this week, Lord. Lord, everything just seems to be crumbling all around me. Lord, I just got this promotion and I'm excited." You're sharing your heart with God. Believers often ask other Christians if they can tarry in prayer for an hour. I believe most believers can tarry in prayer for an hour if they just learn what it is. Most people think prayer is what they hear on a Sunday morning when the preachers and the pastors get up and they start praying. They say, "I can't do that for an hour." You probably can't. However, will you really say that you can't sit down and have a conversation with God for an hour? Yes, you can. Just talk to Him. Just set aside some time and have a conversation with Him.

Let me take a moment and talk to the young men who might be reading this book. Young people, you don't have to be a certain age to pour out your heart to God. Tell Him, what's going on in school and what's going on in your relationships. Just like you'd talk to your close friends, make time and talk to God the same way. Just be honest. He knows what you're thinking. People try to be super-spiritual when they're praying. He knows what's going on in your mind. He knows you're 16 and your hormones are going crazy. He already knows what's going down. He created you that way. He gave you those hormones. He knows that it's tough being a teenager. He understands all of that. To make sure you understand how much He loves you and desires to talk with you, He sent His son Jesus to earth so that He could be better able to understand what we go through.

We've got to communicate and pour our sincere hearts out to God. We must push out all of that foolishness in our minds about not being able to master the formality of praying. "O God, the Alpha and the Omega, the beginning and the end, the God who was, who is and who is to come, glory." Let me explain something to you: we don't talk to anyone else like that. If most believers would simply begin to converse with God, it would turn their lives around. We've got all these false perceptions about prayer. At the end of the day, we should share with God what happened in all of those hours. Make prayer something that you do on a regular basis. Make it a daily part of your life to talk with Him in your car, in your house, on the job, and at church.

When David was in the Cave of Adullam, he didn't have time to run to a church service. He couldn't find one of those regular, more formal places to worship. The man cave was his personal sanctuary and that's where he meet with God for prayer.

faith

noun

: strong belief or trust in someone or something
: belief in the existence of God : strong religious feelings or beliefs
: a system of religious beliefs[10]

Next, David's man cave stimulated faith in God. Psalm 57: 1-3, particularly verse 3 says He was sent from Heaven and saved me.

---

10   http://www.merriam-webster.com/dictionary/faith

The Lord also used David's experience in the cave of Adullam to stimulate David's faith to be in God and God alone.

See that's the key, in God and God alone. The problem for us is that our faith is also in God and others. God brought David to a place in his life to where the only one he could trust was God and God alone. You see, Psalm 57: 1-3 reveals that his faith at the man cave became greater than his troubles at the cave. In life, we all have troubles, but the key is understanding what role our faith plays in handling our troubles. Are our troubles greater than our faith, or is our faith greater than our troubles? God must bring us to a place in our lives where our faith is always greater than our troubles. There should be nothing that we face in this life that our faith can't bring us through. Why? Our faith in God's ability to deliver us from our troubles should be greater than our difficulties.

We need to start modeling David's posture of faith when he was in the man cave. Our troubles don't have to conquer us. You know how many young people I see and talk to, that allow their troubles to conquer them all the time? They're living under the weight of their troubles. They don't understand what the Bible declares, that we are more than conquerors. We're not a bunch of losers.

Let's look at Romans 8:35-37 (NIV). It says, "Who shall separate us from the love of Christ?" All of us have been through at least one of these situations. "Shall trouble or hardship or persecution or famine or nakedness ..." In modern day vernacular he was saying economic challenges, losing a job, losing a paycheck, things happening – "or danger or sword? As it is written 'For your sake we face death all day long. We are considered as sheep to be slaughtered.'" "No, in all these things we are more than conquerors through him who loved us." Are you a loser or a conqueror? You don't have to be a loser as a believer. You can be without a job and still be a winner in God. People may be telling you you're a loser because you don't have a job, because you lost your house, or you lost your car. You ought to tell them that's a lie straight from the pit of hell. That's not God's truth. The Bible says, "… we are more than conquerors through him who loved us," bottom line. Our faith during hard times is greater than our troubles. David's man cave stimulated great faith in God.

Praise

verb

1.   to express a favorable judgment of: commend
2.   to glorify (a god or saint) especially by the attribution of perfections [11]

David's man cave experience stimulated praise for God. See, it was the direction of the praise. You see, the praise was for the Lord. It had to be. Psalm 57:7-10 reveals David learned to praise God in the midst of all of his troubles. Let's took at verse 7. I want to glean from probably the greatest music director that ever walked the face of this earth, David. Verse 7 says, *"My heart is steadfast, O God. My heart is steadfast."* Pause, stop. Put a thumbtack on that, verse 7. David is declaring first of all that he's spiritually and physically prepared for praise. Notice what it says in verse 7, "My heart is steadfast. O God, my heart is

---

11   http://www.merriam-webster.com/dictionary/praise

steadfast." That word steadfast can also be translated "prepared." I'm ready for praise.

Now the question I want to ask today, are you ready for praise? You see it's one thing to say you're praising and it's another thing to be able to look God in the face and say, "God, I'm ready for praise." Sometimes we're not ready for praise. You can't tell me that you've been out all night in the freaky part of town, and you're ready when you roll up in here on Sunday morning to praise God. You get out the car and come in here and say, "Bless the Lord." You're really not ready to praise Him when you're tired and about to fall out from sleep deprivation. You need to run to God first and repent. Repent means to permanently turn away from your sins, not just on that Sunday because you feel guilty. In order to praise God, you've got to come to Him with a clean heart and clean hands. Can you do that after a night of partying?

David continued with, "I will sing." Notice he was spiritually ready and he was physically ready to sing. Do you know that sometimes we are physically ready to praise God, but we're not spiritually ready for praise? Verse 8 says, "Awake, my glory." When we give glory to God where does it come from? It comes from our soul. It comes from who we are. "Awake my soul, awake. Awake, harp and lyre." David was musically inclined. He was saying bring all the musical instruments to a crescendo in praise to the Lord his God. That's what should go on in the church.

He was spiritually and physically ready. He said, "I will awaken the dawn." You say, "What does that mean?" That means David said, "I'm going to get up so early to praise Him that I'm going to awaken the dawn." That means I'm going to wake up early to give God praise. Are we prepared for praise? You roll up in here and you've been going off this morning, slamming cabinets, slamming doors, slamming your foot on the accelerator pedal. You and your wife had your regular Sunday morning argument and now you arrive at church, ready to praise the Lord. What you all need to do is bring the issue, whatever it is to some form of resolution. You need to sit down and have a family meeting, say "Baby I love you. I love you more than life itself, but we fight every Sunday morning. What can we do as a family to stop all this drama before we go to church?"

Be prepared for praise. Are you prepared? Verse 9 reveals his praise will include going public in front of the world, not just in private. Remember David wasn't at a formal church type of religious service. He wasn't there, but he says in verse 9, "I will praise you, O Lord among the peoples. I will sing praises to you among the nations." David said, "I'm going public with my praise." It's a challenge for most believers. We go to church, but we don't go public and God needs us to go public to be a light to a dark and dying world.

Have you gone public with your praise? Then he says in Verse 10, "For Your love and kindness is great to the heavens and Your truth to the clouds. Verse 10 reveals why he praised him. The Bible said, "For Your love and kindness is great to the heavens and Your truth to the clouds." David is praising God because God is good. Why don't we praise Him? God is good. God has been good to all of us.

Verse 11 reveals where David wanted God to be. Look at verse 11. "Be exalted above the heavens. O God, let your glory be over all the earth." Where does he want God to be? He wants God to be Lord and not an underling. Is God your Lord today or is He your underling? David said God be Lord of my life, even if David wouldn't have asked the Lord God to be Lord over his life he is still Lord. The question is where do you want God to be in your life, your Lord or an underling? An underling means that God works for you. Having Him as your Lord means that you work for Him. Let me give you this illustration about what's going on here. First let me set it up. In verses 5 and 6, David is talking about the difficult situation he's in. In verse 7, he just changes direction and says, "I'm steadfast. I'm prepared. I'm ready." He was also saying, "I'm alone." Verse 5 and 6, "I'm hurting" and then he says, "But I'm ready."

We discussed change in an earlier chapter, now let's look at it from a sports viewpoint. One of the hardest things to do mentally and physically in sports is to change direction. Great athletes make it look easy but to be going full speed and to change up like those guys do, that's hard. It looks easy on television, but most of us if not all of us couldn't do that. We would stumble and fall. It takes years of training, trying and falling in order to learn how to change direction. One of the hardest things to do spiritually is to change direction — check this out — from problem to praise. You see, our focus often is on our problem when our focus ought to be on praise. That's a change in direction.

Back in the day there was a play that happened in basketball that I'm still mourning over. It hurts me every time I watch it. In fact, one day Brother Cotton, one of the elders in the church, pulled it up on the Internet and you all know I'm not a violent dude but I really wanted to break his computer screen because he knew he was messing with me. A long time ago there was this guy named Michael Jordan who was a superb basketball player. Then you had some other super stars: John Starks, Oakley, and Patrick Ewing under the basket covering Jordan. Jordan was going in one direction and Oakley and Starks were strategically positioned to block Jordan as he was driving the ball. Oakley comes, cuts off the baseline and Jordan switched directions and successfully scored for his team. He said, "That's a problem," and He changed his course to correct it.

Changing his direction turned his problem into praise. If we would only learn to get our minds to process God's ability to do more than just one move to get us past our problems, we would operate as more than conquerors on a regular basis. Doing a multiplicity of moves so that we can get our direction changed from focusing on our problems takes prayer, faith and praise. Communicating with God on a regular basis can change your direction and turn your problem into praise. That's what David did.

We can't do anything about the things we worry about. Why don't you just change your direction and say, "God, that problem I'm leaving for you because you can handle all of this." I'm changing my direction from a problem focus to praise focus." In the midst of all of your troubles, problems, and pain, praise God. Then you can be victorious in your Cave Adullam experience.

WHAT DOES LOVE
HAVE TO DO WITH IT?

If I speak with the tongues of men and of angels, but do not have love, I have become a noisy gong or a clanging cymbal. If I have the gift of prophecy, and know all mysteries and all knowledge; and if I have all faith, so as to remove mountains, but do not have love, I am nothing. And if I give all my possessions to feed the poor, and if I surrender my body to be burned, but do not have love, it profits me nothing.

Love is patient, love is kind and is not jealous; love does not brag and is not arrogant, does not act unbecomingly; it does not seek its own, is not provoked, does not take into account a wrong suffered, does not rejoice in unrighteousness, but rejoices with the truth; bears all things, believes all things, hopes all things, endures all things.

Love never fails; but if there are gifts of prophecy, they will be done away; if there are tongues, they will cease; if there is knowledge, it will be done away. For we know in part and we prophesy in part; but when the perfect comes, the partial will be done away. When I was a child, I used to speak like a child, think like a child, reason like a child; when I became a man, I did away with childish things. For now we see in a mirror dimly, but then face to face; now I know in part, but then I will know fully just as I also have been fully known. But now faith, hope, love, abide these three; but the greatest of these is love. (1 Corinthians 13)

CHAPTER TEN

DEVELOPING A MAN CAVE MENTALITY

love

noun

1. a profoundly tender, passionate affection for another person.
2. a feeling of warm personal attachment or deep affection, as for a parent, child, or friend.
3. sexual passion or desire.
4. a person toward whom love is felt; beloved person; sweetheart.
5. (used in direct address as a term of endearment, affection, or the like): Would you like to see a movie, love?[12]

---

12   http://dictionary.reference.com/browse/love

The chorus of Tina Turner's song, *What's Love Got To Do With It*, is ringing in my ears as we come to the closing chapter of this book. Let's take a look at what caused a man who was a fugitive with a very dark future to submit to God. Others would have thought during a time like this that He had forsaken them. I propose that David did what he did in the Cave of Adullam because he genuinely loved God.

Now let's get real, David was not a perfect man in any way. He was an adulterer, a liar, a murderer, and covetous. He taught his men discipline but failed to sometimes chastise his own children. He was sometimes disobedient, he took a census of the people willfully disregarding God's instruction not to do that. When you look at his lists of failures, you just might be reminded of your own past. But God! Remember that God is not a respecter of persons, what he did for David, he will do for you if you assume the man cave mentality.

David loved God with all his heart, he loved his laws, he loved his people, and he loved his God assignment. He loved God so much that he was genuinely sorry for his sins and true repentance was a way of life for him when he missed God. You don't believe me? Well, let's take a look at what God said about David at his coronation. In Acts 13:22b, it says, *"After He had removed him [Saul], He raised up David to be their king, concerning whom He also testified and said, 'I HAVE FOUND DAVID the son of Jesse, A MAN AFTER MY HEART, who will do all My will.'"* You can't get any closer to God than that! In Psalm 91:14, God declares the reason why David was lifted up above his enemies. He said, *"Because he has loved Me, therefore,*

I will deliver him [David]; I will set him securely on high, because he has known My name."

When you have an intimate relationship with someone, they know your name and you know theirs. David communed with God on a regular basis. He rose early in the morning in the Cave of Adullam to consult with God. As priests of your household, early morning prayer is the key to establishing order in the lives of your family. Getting your marching orders from God first thing in the morning is critical to the success of your day, it's the posture of kings and warriors who are mighty men of God. Assume the position!

In the book of Psalms, David tells us on numerous accounts about his love for God. I'll share a few of those with you. In Psalm 18:1, he praised the Lord for giving him deliverance from Saul: [For *the choir director. A Psalm of David the servant of the Lord, who spoke to the Lord the words of this song in the day that the Lord delivered him from the hand of all his enemies and from the hand of Saul. And he said,*] "I love You, O Lord, my strength." David is in the midst of praising God when he says this in Psalm 145:20, *The Lord keeps all who love Him, But all the wicked He will destroy.* David knew he was on God's good side because he was faithful to maintain a relationship with Him.

David loved Saul regardless of his attempts to kill him and his forced exile. Saul made his life pretty miserable for 15 years. He killed people he loved and respected and terrorized anyone who even remotely had anything to do with him until his suicide. In 1 Samuel 24:6, we see the extent of that love. When David and Saul were in the cave, he had a chance to end his troubles, but instead he chose to honor Saul's position of authority and spared his life. The scripture states, "And he said unto his men, The Lord forbid that I should do this thing unto my master, the Lord's anointed, to stretch forth mine hand against him, seeing he is the anointed of the Lord." After Saul leaves the cave he calls out to him from a hill where he falls on his face to honor the man of God and pleads his case. David is hoping that Saul will come to his senses and see his true heart's intent to serve him as need be until God makes him king. See before all of this madness Saul was like a surrogate father to David. 1 Samuel 16:21 validates their earlier relationship, *"Then David came to Saul and attended him; and Saul loved him greatly, and he became his armor bearer."*

David loved his friends with a fierce kind of affection. In the midst of a lot of chaos at the palace of Saul, he found solace in a relationship with Saul's oldest son Jonathan. We get a glimpse into that relationship in 1 Samuel 18:1, "*[Jonathan and David]* Now it came about when he had finished speaking to Saul, that the soul of Jonathan was knit to the soul of David, and Jonathan loved him as himself. " When David was forced to flee Saul's palace, where he had been abiding since the age of 15, Jonathan was furious at his father. He had become like an older brother to David. If you remember earlier at his fight with Goliath, David's brothers weren't so fond of him. His older brother taunted him and doubted his ability to kill the giant. In 1 Samuel 20:41 – 42 we see evidence of their love and commitment to one another, *"When the lad was gone, David rose from the south side and fell on his face to the ground, and bowed three times [to Jonathan]. And they kissed each other and wept together, but David wept the more. Jonathan said to David, "Go in safety, inasmuch as we have sworn to each other in the name of the LORD, saying, 'The LORD will be between me and you, and between my descendants and your descendants forever.'"* David lives up to his agreement when he becomes king and finds the only living son of Jonathan, Mephibosheth and brings him to his home and treats him as one of his sons.

David was loved by his people. After Saul's 42 year reign over Israel where the people were distressed, indebted, and discontented, his reign was refreshing. After all, he was a man after God's own heart. 1 Samuel 18:16 says, *"But all Israel and Judah loved David, and he went out and came in before them."* But David could not come into a country that was divided and unite them in their affection for him if he were not a man who loved God.

Loving God is the prerequisite for being able to live a successful life in your personal Cave of Adullam. When it appeared that all was lost for David, he held on to his God, his God promise, and his love for God. Before you can assume any of the other postures, you must first assume the man cave posture of love. 1 Peter 4:8 commands us to put on love, *"Above all, keep fervent in your love for one another, because love covers a multitude of sins."* As a result all that wrong that David did was covered in his love for God and once he was repentant, he was restored back in right relationship with God. God's love for us is extended far beyond what we've done. His grace covers us as we find our way back to him. Love compels us to assume the man cave position. David knew that and was an overcomer in every situation and obstacle he faced. So when you put on the man cave posture of safety; discipline; walking in your anointing;

relief; loyalty; discernment; and prayer, faith, and praise make sure you check your heart to see where you stand in your love relationship with God. Then and only then will you be able to posture yourself for the David kind of success that makes you a king in your area of influence, regardless of your past. Assume the Position, NOW!

ABOUT THE AUTHOR

Michael A. Pender, Sr. is the Founding Pastor of Fallbrook Church in Houston, Texas, where over four thousand families gather each week for worship and sound teaching. He was raised in the Bronx, New York and moved to Houston in 1985, where he continued his education at Houston Baptist University.

Pastor Pender believes the greatest model for leadership is found in Jesus Christ and, therefore, believes in servant-leadership. He believes that his calling is to be a good shepherd over the sheep entrusted to his care at Fallbrook Church.

Pastor Pender is married to Janice Foreman Pender, and they are the proud parents of four children: Bailee, Michael Jr., Arnelle and Colin.

For more information about Pastor Mike or Fallbrook Church go to www.fallbrookchurch.org